Introducti in Banking and Finance

A Non-Technical Handbook for Absolute Beginners

Ramadas B

Copyrights©: Yashas Publications

Preface

Welcome to *Introduction to Blockchain in Banking and Finance: A Non-Technical Handbook for Absolute Beginners*.

As we stand on the brink of a new financial era, blockchain technology is reshaping how we think about transactions, security, and trust in the banking and finance sectors. For many, however, the complexities of blockchain can feel daunting. This book aims to bridge that gap, offering a clear and accessible entry point for anyone eager to understand the fundamental principles of blockchain without getting lost in technical jargon.

In this handbook, we will explore the core concepts of blockchain technology and its applications in the financial landscape. Whether you are a banking professional, an IT enthusiast, a finance student, or simply curious about this transformative technology, this book is designed for you. We will unpack how blockchain works, the key benefits it brings to banking and finance, and how it is already making waves in payment systems, asset management, and regulatory compliance.

Our goal is to demystify blockchain and provide you with practical insights that you can apply in your professional journey. You'll find straightforward explanations, real-world examples, and practical scenarios that illustrate the relevance of blockchain in everyday financial operations.

By the end of this book, you will not only have a solid understanding of blockchain technology but also be equipped to engage in conversations about its implications for the future of banking and finance.

Thank you for embarking on this journey with us. Together, we will navigate the exciting world of blockchain and unlock its potential for transforming the financial industry.

Happy reading!

Table of Contents

Sl. No	Topics	Page No.
1.	**Introduction to Blockchain Technology**	1
	1.1 **What is Blockchain?:** *Basic concepts and definitions of blockchain technology*	10
	1.2 **How Blockchain Works:** *Explanation of blockchain's structure, including blocks, chains, and consensus mechanisms*	15
	1.3 **Blockchain vs. Traditional Databases:** *Key differences between blockchain technology and traditional databases*	21
	1.4 **Basic blockchain framework:** *Core basic components of blockchain framework*	28
	1.5 **Basic blockchain workflow:** *Stages of blockchain in banking and finance*	33
2.	**Blockchain Fundamentals for Banking**	37
	2.1 **Decentralization Explained:** *How decentralization impacts traditional banking systems*	43

	2.2	**Blockchain's Role in Banking:** *The potential applications of blockchain technology in banking services*	50
	2.3	**Basic Terminology:** *Key blockchain terms and concepts relevant to banking professionals*	55
3.	**Blockchain for Secure Transactions**		**60**
	3.1	**How Blockchain Secures Transactions:** *Mechanisms that ensure transaction security and integrity*	66
	3.2	**Cryptographic Principles:** *Introduction to cryptography techniques used in blockchain for securing data*	70
4.	**Smart Contracts and Their Applications**		**74**
	4.1	**What Are Smart Contracts?:** *Basic concept of smart contracts and how they work on blockchain platforms*	79
	4.2	**Benefits of Smart Contracts in Finance:** *Advantages of using smart contracts in financial services*	83
5.	**Blockchain in Payments and Transfers**		**87**
	5.1	**Blockchain for Payment Processing:** *How blockchain*	92

		technology improves payment processing efficiency	
	5.2	**Cross-Border Transfers:** *Benefits of blockchain for international money transfers*	96
	5.3	**Digital Currencies:** *Overview of digital currencies and their role in blockchain-based payments*	102
6.	**Blockchain in Asset Management**		**107**
	6.1	**Tokenization of Assets:** *How blockchain technology is used to tokenize physical and digital assets*	111
	6.2	**Managing Investments with Blockchain:** *The impact of blockchain on investment management and securities*	115
	6.3	**Real-Time Portfolio Tracking:** *Using blockchain for real-time tracking and transparency in asset management*	121
7.	**Regulatory and Compliance Considerations**		**126**
	7.1	**Regulatory Frameworks for Blockchain:** *Key regulations and standards affecting blockchain in banking and finance*	131
	7.2	**Compliance Challenges:** *Common challenges faced by*	143

		financial institutions in complying with blockchain regulations	
	7.3	**Best Practices for Compliance:** *Steps to ensure compliance with regulatory requirements in blockchain applications*	148
8.	**Blockchain in Fraud Prevention**		**152**
	8.1	**Immutable Records:** *The role of blockchain's immutability in preventing fraudulent activities*	158
9.	**Blockchain Integration in Existing Systems**		**162**
	9.1	**Challenges of Integration:** *Key challenges when integrating blockchain with existing banking and finance systems*	167
	9.2	**Strategies for Successful Integration:** *Best practices for effectively incorporating blockchain into current processes*	172
	9.3	**Impact on Legacy Systems:** *How blockchain affects and interacts with traditional banking systems*	178
10	**Future Trends in Blockchain for Finance**		**183**

	10.1	**Emerging Blockchain Technologies:** *New and emerging technologies in blockchain that could impact the finance sector*	189
	10.2	**Ensuring Security in Blockchain:** *Key practices for maintaining security in blockchain systems*	195
11	**Building Blockchain Knowledge and Skills**		199
	11.1	**Educational Resources:** *Available resources for learning more about blockchain technology*	205
12.	**Real-world example case studies**		**209**
	12.1	Case Study 1: *Implementing Blockchain for Secure Transactions: The Case of JPMorgan Chase*	209
	12.2	Case Study 2: *Smart Contracts in Banking: The Case of BBVA and Its Blockchain-Based Loan Solution*	212
	12.3	Case Study 3: *Revolutionizing Payments and Transfers: The Case of Ripple and Cross-Border Transactions*	215
	12.4	Case Study 4: *Transforming Asset Management with*	218

	Blockchain: The Case of Fidelity Investments	
12.5	Case Study 5: *Regulatory Compliance in Banking: The Case of HSBC and Blockchain*	221
12.6	Case Study 6: *Combating Fraud in Banking: The Case of Santander and Blockchain Technology*	225
12.7	Case Study 7: *Integrating Blockchain into Existing Systems: The Case of JPMorgan Chase*	228
12.8	Case Study 8: *Future Trends in Blockchain for Finance: The Case of Wells Fargo and its Blockchain Innovations*	231
12.9	Case Study 9: *Enhancing Security and Privacy with Blockchain: The Case of Bank of America*	235
12.10	Case Study 10: *Empowering Employees Through Blockchain Education: The Case of HSBC*	239
12.11	Case Study 11: *The Future of Finance: How Santander is Utilizing Blockchain for Cross-Border Transfers*	243
12.12	Case Study 12: *Revolutionizing Payment*	246

	Processing: The Case of Visa and Blockchain Integration	
12.13	Case Study 13: *Blockchain vs. Traditional Databases: Key Differences Explored Through the Case of IBM*	249
12.14	Case Study 14: *Blockchain's Role in Banking: The Case of JPMorgan Chase*	252
12.15	Case Study 15: *Decentralization: How Decentralization Impacts Traditional Banking Systems — The Case of BBVA*	255
12.16	Case Study 16: *How Blockchain Secures Transactions: Mechanisms That Ensure Transaction Security and Integrity — The Case of Ripple*	258
12.17	Case Study 17: *Cryptographic Principles in Blockchain: Securing Data with IBM's Hyperledger Fabric*	262
12.18	Case Study 18: *Revolutionizing Financial Transactions: The Power of Smart Contracts at ChainSafe Systems*	266
12.19	Case Study 19: *Transforming Cross-Border Transfers: The Case of RippleNet*	270

12.20 *Case Study 20: Digital* 274
Currencies and Their Role in
Blockchain-Based Payments:
The Case of JPMorgan Chase

1. Introduction to Blockchain Technology

Blockchain technology is a revolutionary innovation that underpins digital currencies like Bitcoin and extends far beyond into various applications across different industries. At its core, a blockchain is a decentralized and distributed ledger system that securely records transactions across a network of computers.

Each transaction is grouped into a block, and these blocks are linked together in a chronological order to form a chain—a "blockchain." This structure ensures that once data is recorded in a block and added to the chain, it cannot be altered or deleted without altering all subsequent blocks, which requires consensus from the network.

Blockchain technology offers several key functions that can transform banking and financial services, enhancing efficiency, security, and transparency. Here are few of the crucial functions of blockchain in these sectors:

1. Enhanced Security and Fraud Prevention

Blockchain's decentralized and immutable ledger significantly improves security in banking and financial transactions. Each transaction is encrypted and linked to previous ones through cryptographic hashes, creating a tamper-resistant record. This design prevents unauthorized alterations and reduces the risk of fraud by ensuring that transaction data remains secure and unchangeable once recorded.

2. Streamlined Cross-Border Payments

Blockchain technology facilitates faster and more cost-effective cross-border payments. Traditional international transactions often involve multiple intermediaries and currency conversions, leading to delays and high fees. Blockchain allows for direct transfers between parties in different countries by eliminating intermediaries, reducing transaction times from days to minutes, and lowering associated costs.

3. Efficient Trade Finance

In trade finance, blockchain enhances the efficiency and transparency of transactions by providing a secure and immutable record of trade documentation. It streamlines processes such as letter of credit issuance and invoice verification by allowing all parties—exporters, importers, and banks—to access and verify the same documentation in real-time, reducing processing times and minimizing fraud.

4. Automated and Transparent Compliance

Blockchain supports automated compliance and regulatory reporting through smart contracts and transparent ledger entries. Smart contracts automatically enforce compliance rules and execute transactions based on predefined conditions, reducing the risk of human error and ensuring adherence to regulations. The transparent nature of blockchain also allows for easier and more accurate auditing of transactions and regulatory compliance.

5. Improved Asset Management

Blockchain technology transforms asset management by enabling the digital representation and management of assets on a decentralized ledger. This includes tokenization of securities, real estate, and other assets, allowing for fractional ownership and easier transferability. Blockchain enhances transparency in asset ownership and transactions, streamlining processes such as trading, settlement, and custody.

6. Secure and Efficient Digital Identity Verification

Blockchain provides a secure and decentralized method for managing digital identities in banking and financial services. By using blockchain for identity verification, institutions can create tamper-proof and verifiable digital identities for customers. This improves the security and efficiency of onboarding processes, reduces the risk of identity theft, and simplifies Know Your Customer (KYC) and Anti-Money Laundering (AML) compliance.

These functions highlight how blockchain technology can address key challenges in banking and financial services, offering solutions that enhance security, reduce costs, and improve overall efficiency.

The decentralized nature of blockchain means that no single entity has control over the entire ledger, making it resistant to tampering and fraud. Every participant in the network has access to the same information, providing transparency and fostering trust. Transactions are verified through consensus mechanisms such as Proof of Work or Proof of Stake, which ensure the integrity of the data without needing a central authority.

Beyond its application in cryptocurrencies, blockchain technology is transforming various sectors by enhancing security, reducing costs, and improving transparency. It enables the creation of smart contracts—self-executing agreements with terms directly written into code—facilitating automated and trustless interactions between parties. Additionally, blockchain supports innovations in areas such as supply chain management, digital identity verification, and decentralized finance (DeFi), showcasing its versatility and potential to reshape traditional systems and processes.

Here are some examples of how blockchain technology is being used in the banking and finance sectors:

Cross-Border Payments: Blockchain technology simplifies and speeds up cross-border payments by eliminating intermediaries and reducing transaction costs. Traditional international transfers often involve multiple banks and currency exchanges, which can be slow and costly. With blockchain, transactions are recorded on a decentralized ledger, allowing for near-instantaneous and transparent transfers between parties across different countries, thereby enhancing efficiency and reducing fees.

Trade Finance: In trade finance, blockchain streamlines and secures the documentation process involved in global trade transactions. By providing a tamper-proof ledger, blockchain ensures that all parties involved in trade—such as exporters, importers, and financial institutions—have access to the same verified information. This reduces fraud, accelerates processing times, and lowers costs by automating and securing trade documentation and transactions.

Digital Identity Verification: Blockchain enhances digital identity verification by providing a secure and immutable way to store and manage personal identity data. Traditional methods of identity verification can be cumbersome and prone to errors or fraud. Blockchain allows individuals to maintain control over their identity information while providing businesses with a reliable means of verifying identities, thus improving security and efficiency in processes such as account opening and online transactions.

Smart Contracts: Smart contracts are self-executing contracts with the terms directly written into code, which run on blockchain networks. They automatically enforce and execute contract terms when predefined conditions are met, eliminating the need for intermediaries and reducing the risk of disputes. Smart contracts enable automated, transparent, and trustless agreements in various applications, including financial services, real estate, and supply chain management.

Securities Trading: Blockchain technology transforms securities trading by providing a secure and transparent platform for recording and settling trades. By digitizing securities and recording transactions on a decentralized ledger, blockchain improves the speed and accuracy of trading, reduces settlement times from days to minutes, and enhances transparency and auditability, which can lead to increased investor confidence and reduced operational costs.

Fraud Prevention and Compliance: Blockchain enhances fraud prevention and compliance by creating an immutable and transparent record of transactions that can be easily audited. This transparency helps in detecting and preventing fraudulent activities and ensures compliance with regulatory requirements by providing a reliable and verifiable trail of transactions, reducing the risk of data tampering and improving overall trust in financial processes.

Decentralized Finance (DeFi): Decentralized Finance (DeFi) leverages blockchain technology to recreate traditional financial systems, such as lending, borrowing, and trading, on a decentralized platform. DeFi platforms operate without intermediaries, offering open and permissionless access to financial services, and enabling greater financial inclusion and innovation. This shift to decentralized platforms also reduces costs and increases transparency in financial transactions.

KYC (Know Your Customer) and AML (Anti-Money Laundering): Blockchain supports KYC and AML efforts by providing a secure and transparent way to manage and verify customer identities and transactions. Blockchain's immutable ledger allows for efficient tracking and verification of identity documents and transaction histories, aiding in compliance with regulatory requirements and improving the accuracy and efficiency of anti-money laundering processes.

Asset Management: Blockchain technology revolutionizes asset management by offering a secure, transparent, and efficient way to track and manage investments. Through blockchain, asset managers can record ownership and transfer of assets in real-time, reduce administrative costs, and enhance transparency. This technology also facilitates fractional ownership and the creation of digital tokens representing various assets, broadening access to investment opportunities.

Real Estate Transactions: In real estate, blockchain streamlines property transactions by providing a secure and transparent platform for recording property ownership and transfers. By eliminating the need for intermediaries and paper-based processes, blockchain reduces transaction times and costs, enhances the accuracy of property records, and simplifies the process of buying, selling, and transferring real estate assets, thereby increasing efficiency and trust in the real estate market.

Real-world examples:

> Here are the real-world examples of how blockchain technology is being used in the banking and finance sectors:
>
> **1. Cross-Border Payments**
>
> **Example: Ripple (XRP)**
>
> - **Description**: Ripple uses blockchain technology to facilitate faster and more cost-effective cross-border payments. Unlike traditional systems that can take days to process international transactions, Ripple's blockchain-based solution enables near-instantaneous transfers between financial institutions.
> - **Benefits**: Reduces transaction fees and speeds up processing times, providing a more efficient way for banks and financial institutions to handle international payments.
>
> **2. Trade Finance**
>
> **Example: Marco Polo Network**
>
> - **Description**: The Marco Polo Network is a blockchain-based trade finance platform that streamlines and digitizes the process of trade finance, including invoice financing and letters of credit. It connects banks, corporates, and other trade participants on a single platform.

- **Benefits**: Improves transparency, reduces fraud, and accelerates the trade finance process by enabling real-time tracking of transactions and documents.

3. Digital Identity Verification

Example: U-Port

- **Description**: U-Port provides a decentralized digital identity solution based on blockchain technology. Users can manage their personal data and credentials securely and share them with trusted parties without intermediaries.
- **Benefits**: Enhances security and privacy by giving users control over their digital identities and reducing the risk of identity theft and fraud.

4. Smart Contracts

Example: Ethereum

- **Description**: Ethereum's blockchain enables the creation of smart contracts—self-executing contracts with the terms written into code. These contracts automatically execute and enforce agreements once pre-set conditions are met.
- **Benefits**: Automates complex financial transactions, reduces the need for intermediaries, and increases transparency and efficiency in contract execution.

5. Securities Trading

Example: Nasdaq Linq

- **Description**: Nasdaq Linq is a blockchain platform developed by Nasdaq for the issuance, trading, and settlement of private securities. It provides a secure and transparent way to manage securities transactions and ownership.
- **Benefits**: Reduces administrative costs, increases transparency, and enhances the efficiency of securities trading and settlement processes.

6. Fraud Prevention and Compliance

Example: IBM and Stellar

- **Description**: IBM and Stellar are collaborating to use blockchain for cross-border payment solutions and compliance tracking. Their blockchain system aims to enhance security, streamline compliance, and reduce fraud in financial transactions.
- **Benefits**: Enhances fraud detection, ensures regulatory compliance, and improves the security of financial transactions through real-time monitoring and verification.

7. Decentralized Finance (DeFi)

Example: Compound

- **Description**: Compound is a decentralized finance (DeFi) platform built on the Ethereum blockchain that allows users to lend and borrow cryptocurrencies without the need for traditional financial intermediaries. Users earn interest on their deposits and can take out loans against their crypto assets.
- **Benefits**: Provides greater accessibility to financial services, reduces reliance on traditional banks, and allows for more flexible and decentralized financial transactions.

8. KYC (Know Your Customer) and AML (Anti-Money Laundering)

Example: Shyft Network

- **Description**: Shyft Network uses blockchain technology to improve KYC and AML processes. It provides a decentralized identity verification platform that enables secure and efficient customer onboarding and compliance checks.
- **Benefits**: Streamlines KYC and AML compliance, reduces costs associated with manual verification processes, and enhances data security and privacy.

9. Asset Management

Example: Fidelity Digital Assets

- **Description**: Fidelity Digital Assets offers a blockchain-based platform for the custody and management of digital assets, including cryptocurrencies. It provides institutional investors with a secure and compliant solution for managing their digital assets.
- **Benefits**: Enhances security and compliance for institutional investors dealing with digital assets, and facilitates easier and more secure management of cryptocurrency holdings.

10. Real Estate Transactions

Example: Propy

- **Description**: Propy is a blockchain-based platform that facilitates real estate transactions by recording property transfers and ownership on a blockchain. It aims to simplify the buying and selling process for real estate by digitizing and automating key aspects of the transaction.
- **Benefits**: Increases transparency, reduces paperwork, and speeds up real estate transactions by leveraging blockchain technology to record and verify ownership and transaction details.

These real-world examples illustrate how blockchain technology is transforming various aspects of the banking and finance industries, from cross-border payments and trade finance to digital identity verification and decentralized finance. By leveraging blockchain's key characteristics—such as decentralization, transparency, and immutability—these applications are improving efficiency, security, and transparency in financial operations.

1.1 What is Blockchain?: *Basic concepts and definitions of blockchain technology*

Blockchain technology, a decentralized and distributed ledger system, has gained significant attention across various sectors due to its potential to enhance transparency, security, and efficiency.

Initially popularized by cryptocurrencies like Bitcoin, blockchain's applications extend far beyond digital currencies, influencing fields such as supply chain management, healthcare, finance, and more.

1. What is Blockchain?

a. Definition and Basic Concept

- **Blockchain**: A blockchain is a type of distributed ledger that records transactions across a network of computers in a secure, immutable way. Each transaction, or "block," is linked to the previous one, forming a "chain" of blocks.

- **Key Characteristics**:
    - **Decentralization**: Unlike traditional ledgers, blockchain operates on a decentralized network, meaning no single entity has control over the entire system.
    - **Transparency**: All participants in the network have access to the entire ledger, enhancing transparency.
    - **Immutability**: Once data is recorded in a block, it cannot be altered or deleted, ensuring the integrity of the information.
    - **Consensus Mechanisms**: Transactions are validated through consensus protocols, such as Proof of Work (PoW) or Proof of Stake (PoS), ensuring that all participants agree on the validity of transactions.

b. Components of a Blockchain

- **Blocks**: Each block contains a list of transactions, a timestamp, and a reference (hash) to the previous block.
- **Chain**: Blocks are linked sequentially to form a chain, with each block containing a hash of the previous block.
- **Nodes**: Computers participating in the network that validate and relay transactions.
- **Consensus Protocols**: Algorithms used to agree on the validity of transactions and maintain the integrity of the blockchain.

2. Types of Blockchain

a. Public Blockchain

- **Description**: Open to anyone who wants to participate and validate transactions. Examples include Bitcoin and Ethereum.

- **Pros**: High security and transparency, as anyone can verify transactions.
- **Cons**: Can be slow and resource-intensive due to the need for widespread consensus.

b. Private Blockchain

- **Description**: Restricted to a specific group of participants with permission to access and validate transactions. Examples include Hyperledger Fabric and R3 Corda.
- **Pros**: Faster transaction processing and more control over access and permissions.
- **Cons**: Less transparency compared to public blockchains, as access is limited to authorized participants.

c. Consortium Blockchain

- **Description**: Controlled by a group of organizations or entities rather than a single one. Examples include the Enterprise Ethereum Alliance (EEA) and the Energy Web Foundation.
- **Pros**: Balance between transparency and control, as multiple organizations collaborate to manage the blockchain.
- **Cons**: May face challenges related to trust and coordination among consortium members.

4. Benefits of Blockchain Technology

- **Security**: Cryptographic techniques ensure data integrity and security.
- **Transparency**: All participants have access to the same data, enhancing trust and accountability.
- **Efficiency**: Reduces the need for intermediaries and speeds up transaction processing.
- **Decentralization**: Eliminates the single point of failure, making systems more resilient.

5. Challenges and Considerations

- **Scalability**: Blockchain networks can face scalability issues, particularly with high transaction volumes.
- **Regulation**: The regulatory environment for blockchain technology is still evolving, which can impact its adoption and implementation.
- **Energy Consumption**: Certain consensus mechanisms, like Proof of Work, can be energy-intensive, raising environmental concerns.
- **Interoperability**: Integrating different blockchain systems and ensuring they can work together effectively remains a challenge.

6. Applications of Blockchain Technology

a. Cryptocurrencies
- **Example**: Bitcoin, Ethereum – Digital currencies that use blockchain to record and verify transactions.

b. Supply Chain Management
- **Example**: IBM Food Trust – Tracks the provenance of food products through the supply chain, enhancing transparency and traceability.

c. Healthcare
- **Example**: MediLedger – A blockchain-based platform for tracking and verifying pharmaceuticals to prevent counterfeiting and ensure safety.

d. Smart Contracts
- **Example**: Ethereum – Facilitates the creation of self-executing contracts with the terms written into code, automatically executing when conditions are met.

e. Voting Systems
- **Example**: Voatz – Uses blockchain to provide secure and transparent voting solutions, aiming to increase election integrity and voter participation.

Summary

Blockchain technology represents a transformative shift in how data is recorded, verified, and managed across various sectors. Its core principles of decentralization, transparency, and immutability offer numerous benefits, from enhancing security to increasing efficiency. As blockchain technology continues to evolve, its applications are expanding, with potential impacts on finance, supply chain management, healthcare, and beyond. Understanding the fundamental concepts, benefits, and challenges of blockchain provides a foundation for exploring its applications and innovations in various industries.

1.2 How Blockchain Works: *Explanation of blockchain's structure, including blocks, chains, and consensus mechanisms*

Blockchain technology is a foundational element for decentralized systems, providing a secure and transparent way to record and verify transactions.

Here's a detailed explanation of its structure, including blocks, chains, and consensus mechanisms, followed by real-world examples illustrating its application.

1. Blockchain Structure

a. Blocks

- **Definition**: A block is a unit of data that contains a collection of transactions. Each block typically consists of:
    o **Header**: Contains metadata about the block, including a timestamp and a reference to the previous block.
    o **Transactions**: A list of transactions that have occurred and are recorded within this block.
    o **Hash**: A unique digital fingerprint for the block. It is generated based on the block's contents, ensuring the block's integrity.
- **Example**: In a Bitcoin blockchain, a block might include a set of Bitcoin transactions where users transfer Bitcoin from one address to another.

b. Chain

- **Definition**: The chain is a sequential linkage of blocks. Each block contains a hash of the previous block, creating a continuous and immutable chain of blocks.
- **Function**: This linkage ensures that once data is recorded in a block, it cannot be altered without changing all subsequent blocks, which requires consensus from the network.
- **Example**: In a blockchain used for supply chain management, each block records the movement of goods through different stages, forming a chain that provides a transparent history of the product's journey.

c. Consensus Mechanisms

Consensus mechanisms are protocols used to achieve agreement on the validity of transactions and the state of the blockchain among distributed nodes (computers) in the network. Here are some common consensus mechanisms:

- **Proof of Work (PoW)**
    o **Description**: Requires participants (miners) to solve complex cryptographic puzzles to validate

transactions and add new blocks to the blockchain.
- **Example**: Bitcoin uses PoW, where miners compete to solve mathematical problems, and the first to solve it gets to add the new block to the blockchain.

- **Proof of Stake (PoS)**
  - **Description**: Validators are chosen to create new blocks based on the amount of cryptocurrency they hold and are willing to "stake" as collateral.
  - **Example**: Ethereum 2.0 plans to use PoS, where validators are selected to propose and validate blocks based on their stake, reducing energy consumption compared to PoW.

- **Delegated Proof of Stake (DPoS)**
  - **Description**: Stakeholders elect delegates who validate transactions and create new blocks on their behalf. This system aims to increase efficiency and scalability.
  - **Example**: EOS uses DPoS, where token holders vote for block producers who are responsible for maintaining the blockchain.

- **Practical Byzantine Fault Tolerance (PBFT)**
  - **Description**: Achieves consensus by allowing nodes to reach agreement even if some nodes fail or act maliciously. It is used in permissioned blockchains.
  - **Example**: Hyperledger Fabric employs PBFT, ensuring that even with a fraction of nodes potentially being faulty or dishonest, the network can still agree on the validity of transactions.

How Blockchain Works

a. Transaction Initiation

- **Step**: A transaction is initiated and broadcasted to the network. For example, sending cryptocurrency from one wallet to another.

b. Transaction Validation

- **Step**: Nodes in the network validate the transaction using consensus mechanisms. For public blockchains, this might involve solving complex cryptographic puzzles (Proof of Work) or proving ownership of staked assets (Proof of Stake).

c. Block Creation

- **Step**: Validated transactions are grouped into a block. The block contains a cryptographic hash of the previous block, linking it to the existing chain.

d. Consensus and Addition

- **Step**: Once consensus is reached, the new block is added to the blockchain. The updated blockchain is then distributed to all nodes in the network.

e. Immutable Record

Step: The transaction is permanently recorded in the blockchain, making it immutable and tamper-proof.

2. Real-World Examples

a. Cross-Border Payments

- **Example**: **Ripple (XRP)**
  o **Description**: Ripple's blockchain facilitates instant and cost-effective cross-border payments. It uses a consensus algorithm called the Ripple Protocol Consensus Algorithm (RPCA) to validate transactions and achieve agreement without relying on mining.
  o **Impact**: Significantly reduces transaction fees and processing times compared to traditional banking systems.

b. **Supply Chain Management**
- **Example**: IBM Food Trust
    - **Description**: IBM Food Trust utilizes blockchain to track the journey of food products from farm to table. Each block in the chain records detailed information about the product's movement and condition.
    - **Impact**: Enhances transparency, reduces fraud, and improves traceability in the food supply chain, leading to higher safety and efficiency.

c. **Digital Identity Verification**
- **Example**: U-Port
    - **Description**: U-Port provides a decentralized digital identity system using blockchain. Users create and manage their digital identities securely, with their information stored in blocks across the network.
    - **Impact**: Simplifies identity verification processes, enhances security, and reduces identity theft risks.

d. **Securities Trading**
- **Example**: Nasdaq Linq
    - **Description**: Nasdaq Linq uses blockchain technology to record and manage private securities transactions. Each transaction is recorded in a block, linked to previous transactions, and validated by a network of participants.
    - **Impact**: Streamlines the issuance, trading, and settlement of securities, improving transparency and reducing administrative costs.

e. Decentralized Finance (DeFi)

- **Example**: Compound
    - **Description**: Compound is a DeFi platform that uses blockchain to facilitate lending and borrowing of cryptocurrencies. Smart contracts on the blockchain manage transactions and interest rates automatically.
    - **Impact**: Provides a decentralized alternative to traditional financial services, allowing users to earn interest on their crypto holdings and borrow assets without intermediaries.

Summary

Blockchain technology operates through a well-defined structure involving blocks, chains, and consensus mechanisms to ensure secure, transparent, and immutable record-keeping. The integration of various consensus algorithms enhances the efficiency and scalability of the blockchain network. Real-world applications across sectors such as cross-border payments, supply chain management, digital identity verification, and securities trading showcase blockchain's transformative potential, demonstrating its ability to improve processes and reduce costs in various industries.

1.3 Blockchain vs. Traditional Databases:
Key differences between blockchain technology and traditional databases

Blockchain technology and traditional databases serve different purposes and have distinct characteristics.

Here's a comparison highlighting their key differences:

1. Data Structure

- **Blockchain**:
    - **Structure**: Data is organized into blocks that are linked together in a chronological chain. Each block contains a set of transactions and a reference (hash) to the previous block, creating a secure and immutable ledger.

- **Immutability**: Once data is added to a block and the block is linked to the chain, it cannot be altered without changing all subsequent blocks, which requires consensus from the network.

- **Traditional Database**:
    - **Structure**: Data is stored in tables with rows and columns. Each table can be updated or deleted independently of others.
    - **Mutability**: Data can be modified, updated, or deleted as needed, and changes are generally recorded in real-time.

2. Centralization vs. Decentralization

- **Blockchain**:
    - **Decentralization**: Data is distributed across a network of nodes (computers). Each node has a copy of the blockchain, and transactions are verified by consensus among multiple nodes.
    - **Trust Model**: Trust is established through cryptographic proofs and consensus mechanisms rather than relying on a central authority.

- **Traditional Database**:
    - **Centralization**: Data is typically managed by a central server or database administrator. Access and control are centralized within the organization.
    - **Trust Model**: Trust is based on the integrity of the central authority or administrator managing the database.

3. Consensus Mechanisms

- **Blockchain**:
    - **Consensus Mechanisms**: Blockchain uses various consensus algorithms (e.g., Proof of Work, Proof of Stake, Practical Byzantine Fault

Tolerance) to validate and agree on the state of the ledger. This process ensures that all participants have a consistent view of the data.
    - **Example**: Bitcoin uses Proof of Work, where miners solve cryptographic puzzles to validate transactions and add blocks to the chain.
- **Traditional Database**:
    - **No Consensus**: Traditional databases rely on single-point authority and do not use consensus mechanisms. Transactions are validated and processed by the central server or database management system.
    - **Example**: In a relational database, transactions are managed by the database management system (DBMS) with mechanisms such as ACID properties (Atomicity, Consistency, Isolation, Durability) for maintaining data integrity.

4. Transparency and Privacy

- **Blockchain**:
    - **Transparency**: Public blockchains are transparent, allowing anyone to view the entire transaction history and verify the data. Private blockchains have restricted access but still maintain transparency within the network.
    - **Privacy**: Privacy can be enhanced using encryption and pseudonymous addresses. However, transparency can sometimes compromise privacy depending on the blockchain's design.
- **Traditional Database**:
    - **Transparency**: Traditional databases do not offer inherent transparency. Access is controlled by permissions and access controls set by the database administrator.

- **Privacy**: Privacy is managed through access controls, authentication, and encryption but is centralized, relying on the security measures of the database management system.

5. Scalability and Performance

- **Blockchain**:
  - **Scalability**: Blockchains can face scalability challenges due to the need for consensus and the growing size of the ledger. Performance can be slower compared to traditional databases due to the decentralized nature and cryptographic operations.
  - **Example**: Bitcoin's blockchain has relatively slow transaction processing times due to the Proof of Work consensus mechanism.
- **Traditional Database**:
  - **Scalability**: Traditional databases are often more scalable and can handle a high volume of transactions with faster performance. They can be scaled vertically (upgrading hardware) or horizontally (adding more servers).
  - **Example**: SQL databases like MySQL and NoSQL databases like MongoDB can be optimized for high-performance scenarios and handle large-scale data efficiently.

6. Use Cases

- **Blockchain**:
  - **Use Cases**: Ideal for scenarios requiring decentralized trust, immutability, and transparency. Commonly used for cryptocurrencies, supply chain tracking, digital identity verification, and smart contracts.

- o **Example**: Ethereum's smart contracts enable automated agreements and transactions without intermediaries.
- **Traditional Database**:
  - o **Use Cases**: Suitable for applications requiring centralized control, rapid updates, and complex querying capabilities. Commonly used for enterprise data management, customer relationship management (CRM), and financial transactions.
  - o **Example**: Oracle Database is used by large organizations for enterprise resource planning (ERP) and business intelligence.

Real-world examples:

Here are few real-world examples that illustrate the differences between blockchain technology and traditional databases across various industries:

1. Cryptocurrencies (Blockchain)
• **Example: Bitcoin**
o **Description:** Bitcoin utilizes a decentralized blockchain to facilitate peer-to-peer transactions without intermediaries. The blockchain records all transactions in an immutable ledger, ensuring transparency and security. Each transaction must be validated by miners through the Proof of Work consensus mechanism, which prevents tampering.
2. Supply Chain Management (Blockchain)
• **Example: IBM Food Trust**
o **Description:** IBM Food Trust uses blockchain technology to enhance transparency and traceability in the food supply chain. Participants, including farmers, processors, distributors, and retailers, share access to a

single, immutable ledger that tracks the journey of food products from farm to table. This reduces fraud, ensures food safety, and enhances trust among stakeholders.

3. **Customer Relationship Management (CRM) (Traditional Database)**
   - **Example: Salesforce**
     - **Description:** Salesforce is a widely-used traditional CRM system that relies on centralized databases to manage customer interactions and data. It allows organizations to update customer records in real time, run complex queries, and analyze customer data for insights. Its centralized nature ensures quick access and updates but does not offer the immutability of blockchain.

4. **Healthcare Data Management (Traditional Database)**
   - **Example: Epic Systems**
     - **Description:** Epic Systems provides electronic health record (EHR) solutions for hospitals and healthcare providers, utilizing traditional databases for patient data management. The centralized system allows for efficient data entry, retrieval, and updates, but relies on access controls to ensure privacy and security of sensitive health information.

5. **Smart Contracts (Blockchain)**
   - **Example: Ethereum**
     - **Description:** Ethereum's blockchain supports smart contracts, which are self-executing contracts with the terms of the agreement directly written into code. These contracts operate without intermediaries, automatically executing transactions when predefined conditions are met. This use case exemplifies

	blockchain's capability for automation, transparency, and trust in decentralized environments.

These examples highlight the distinct applications of blockchain and traditional databases in real-world scenarios. Blockchain shines in environments requiring decentralization, transparency, and immutability, while traditional databases excel in centralized control, performance, and rapid updates for complex data management tasks. Each technology plays a vital role in its respective use cases, underscoring their unique strengths and functionalities.

Summary

Blockchain technology differs from traditional databases in several fundamental ways, including data structure, centralization, consensus mechanisms, transparency, privacy, scalability, and use cases. Blockchain offers a decentralized and immutable ledger with enhanced security and transparency, making it suitable for applications that require these features. Traditional databases, on the other hand, provide centralized control with faster performance and greater scalability, making them suitable for a wide range of business applications. Each technology has its own strengths and is suited to different types of use cases.

1.4 Basic blockchain framework: *Core basic components of blockchain framework*

A blockchain framework designed for banking and finance revolves around core principles of distributed ledger technology, cryptographic security, and consensus mechanisms.

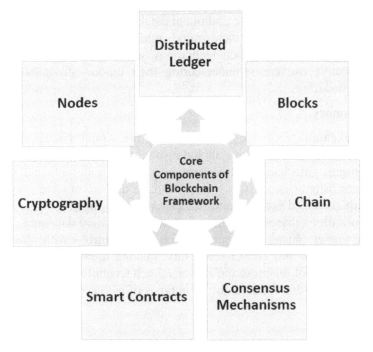

Below is a structured overview of how blockchain can be applied in these sectors, focusing on its basic framework and key components.

1. Core Components of Blockchain Framework

a. **Distributed Ledger**

- **Definition**: A decentralized database where records are maintained across multiple nodes in a network.
- **Function in Banking**: Ensures transparency and immutability of financial transactions across all participating institutions.

b. **Blocks**
- **Definition**: Data structures that hold transaction records and other relevant information.
- **Function in Banking**: Each block contains details of multiple transactions and is linked to the previous block, creating a chain.

c. **Chain**
- **Definition**: The continuous sequence of blocks, each referencing the previous block via a cryptographic hash.
- **Function in Banking**: Maintains a secure and immutable record of all transactions.

d. **Consensus Mechanisms**
- **Definition**: Algorithms used to agree on the state of the blockchain and validate new transactions.
- **Types**:
    - **Proof of Work (PoW)**: Nodes solve cryptographic puzzles to validate transactions (e.g., Bitcoin).
    - **Proof of Stake (PoS)**: Validators are chosen based on their stake or investment in the network (e.g., Ethereum 2.0).
    - **Practical Byzantine Fault Tolerance (PBFT)**: Nodes reach consensus through voting and agreement on transaction validity.
- **Function in Banking**: Ensures that all participants in the network agree on the accuracy of transactions and maintain the integrity of the blockchain.

e. **Smart Contracts**
- **Definition**: Self-executing contracts with terms written in code that automatically execute and enforce agreements.

- **Function in Banking**: Automates complex financial transactions and agreements, reducing the need for intermediaries.

f. **Cryptography**
- **Definition**: Techniques used to secure information through encryption and decryption.
- **Function in Banking**: Protects the integrity and confidentiality of transaction data.

g. **Nodes**
- **Definition**: Computers or servers that participate in the blockchain network, validating and propagating transactions.
- **Function in Banking**: Each node maintains a copy of the blockchain ledger and contributes to consensus.

2. *Blockchain Framework in Banking and Finance*

a. **Transaction Processing**
- **Step 1**: Initiation - A transaction is initiated by a party (e.g., a payment transfer).
- **Step 2**: Broadcasting - The transaction is broadcasted to the network for validation.
- **Step 3**: Validation - Nodes validate the transaction using consensus mechanisms.
- **Step 4**: Recording - The validated transaction is recorded in a new block.
- **Step 5**: Confirmation - The block is added to the blockchain, and the transaction is confirmed.

b. **Identity and Access Management**
- **Decentralized Identity**: Blockchain can provide secure, verifiable digital identities for users.
- **Access Control**: Blockchain can manage and control access to financial services and data based on user permissions and roles.

c. **Regulatory Compliance**
- **Audit Trails**: Blockchain provides immutable records for compliance and audit purposes.
- **Smart Contracts**: Automate compliance checks and reporting requirements.

d. **Interbank Transfers**
- **Cross-Border Payments**: Blockchain can streamline international transactions by reducing intermediaries and transaction times.
- **Settlement Systems**: Real-time settlement of trades and transactions improves efficiency and reduces risks.

3. Real-World Examples

a. **Ripple**
- **Description**: Ripple provides a blockchain-based platform for real-time cross-border payments.
- **Use Case**: RippleNet enables banks to send money across borders quickly and at lower costs by utilizing a distributed ledger.

b. **JPMorgan Chase's JPM Coin**
- **Description**: JPM Coin is a digital token developed by JPMorgan Chase to facilitate instantaneous payments between institutional clients.
- **Use Case**: It leverages blockchain technology for secure and efficient intra-bank transfers.

c. **IBM Blockchain for Trade Finance**
- **Description**: IBM's blockchain solutions are used to streamline trade finance processes, including supply chain and letter of credit transactions.
- **Use Case**: Reduces paperwork and accelerates transaction processing through a shared ledger.

d. **Deutsche Bank's Blockchain-Based Trade Finance**

- **Description**: Deutsche Bank uses blockchain technology for digitizing and automating trade finance processes.
- **Use Case**: Enhances transparency and reduces fraud in trade finance transactions.

e. **Standard Chartered and Linklogis**
- **Description**: Standard Chartered collaborates with Linklogis to develop blockchain solutions for supply chain finance.
- **Use Case**: Improves supply chain finance efficiency and transparency through a distributed ledger.

Summary

The blockchain framework in banking and finance revolves around distributed ledgers, blocks, chains, consensus mechanisms, smart contracts, and cryptography. By implementing these components, financial institutions can enhance transaction security, reduce costs, streamline processes, and ensure regulatory compliance. Real-world examples, such as Ripple, JPM Coin, and IBM Blockchain, demonstrate the practical applications and benefits of blockchain technology in the finance sector.

1.5 Basic blockchain workflow: *Stages of blockchain in banking and finance*

The blockchain workflow in banking and finance involves several stages from transaction initiation to final settlement, ensuring secure, transparent, and efficient processes.

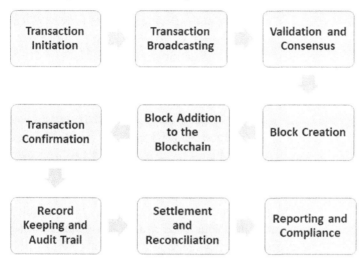

Here's a structured overview of the basic workflow:

1. Transaction Initiation

- **Party Involvement**: A transaction is initiated by a party within the banking or finance system, such as a payment transfer, securities trade, or loan disbursement.
- **Data Input**: Relevant transaction details are input into the system, including the parties involved, amounts, and terms of the transaction.

2. Transaction Broadcasting

- **Broadcasting**: The transaction request is broadcasted to the network of blockchain nodes (computers) that participate in the blockchain.
- **Network Notification**: All nodes in the blockchain network receive the transaction data for validation.

3. Validation and Consensus

- **Validation**: Nodes validate the transaction based on pre-defined rules and consensus mechanisms. This step ensures that the transaction is legitimate and complies with the blockchain protocol.
    - **Consensus Mechanisms**:
        - **Proof of Work (PoW)**: Nodes solve complex cryptographic puzzles to validate the transaction.
        - **Proof of Stake (PoS)**: Nodes are chosen based on their stake in the blockchain network.
        - **Practical Byzantine Fault Tolerance (PBFT)**: Nodes achieve consensus through voting and agreement on transaction validity.
- **Consensus Achievement**: Nodes agree on the validity of the transaction, which is crucial for maintaining the integrity of the blockchain.

4. Block Creation

- **Block Formation**: Validated transactions are grouped into a block by a node or a miner.
- **Block Header**: The block includes a header with a timestamp, previous block's hash, and a nonce (in PoW systems), along with the list of transactions.
- **Hashing**: The block header is hashed to produce a unique block identifier, ensuring data integrity and linking to the previous block in the chain.

5. Block Addition to the Blockchain

- **Propagation**: Once the block is created and validated, it is propagated to other nodes in the network.
- **Block Addition**: The block is added to the existing blockchain by appending it to the end of the chain, and all nodes update their copies of the blockchain ledger.

6. Transaction Confirmation

- **Confirmation**: The transaction is considered confirmed once the block containing it has been added to the blockchain.
- **Multiple Confirmations**: In some systems, multiple confirmations are required to ensure transaction finality and to prevent double-spending.

7. Record Keeping and Audit Trail

- **Immutable Ledger**: The blockchain ledger, now containing the new block, provides an immutable record of the transaction.
- **Audit Trail**: The complete transaction history is available for audit and verification purposes, enhancing transparency and accountability.

8. Settlement and Reconciliation

- **Settlement**: For financial transactions, settlement involves transferring ownership or funds based on the transaction details.
- **Reconciliation**: Transactions are reconciled between involved parties, ensuring that records match and any discrepancies are resolved.

9. Reporting and Compliance

- **Reporting**: Transaction data can be used for regulatory reporting, compliance checks, and internal financial reporting.
- **Compliance**: Ensures adherence to financial regulations and standards by leveraging the transparent and immutable nature of the blockchain.

Real-World Examples

1. **Ripple**
   - **Workflow**: Ripple facilitates cross-border payments by using blockchain to securely and transparently handle international transactions. Transactions are

> broadcasted to the Ripple network, validated, and settled in real-time.
>
> **2. JPM Coin by JPMorgan Chase**
>
> - **Workflow**: JPM Coin is used for instantaneous transfers between institutional clients. Transactions are initiated, validated, and settled using blockchain, with real-time updates and confirmations.
>
> **3. IBM Blockchain for Trade Finance**
>
> - **Workflow**: IBM Blockchain enhances trade finance processes by creating a shared ledger for trade transactions. Transactions are broadcasted, validated, and recorded on the blockchain, improving transparency and efficiency.
>
> **4. Deutsche Bank's Blockchain Trade Finance**
>
> - **Workflow**: Deutsche Bank uses blockchain to digitize trade finance processes, from transaction initiation to settlement. Transactions are recorded on the blockchain, providing a secure and immutable record.
>
> **5. Standard Chartered and Linklogis**
>
> - **Workflow**: Standard Chartered and Linklogis use blockchain for supply chain finance. Transactions are tracked and validated on a blockchain ledger, ensuring transparency and reducing fraud.

Summary

The basic blockchain workflow in banking and finance involves transaction initiation, broadcasting, validation, block creation, addition to the blockchain, transaction confirmation, record-keeping, settlement, and compliance. Real-world examples like Ripple and JPM Coin demonstrate how these workflows are applied to enhance efficiency, security, and transparency in financial transactions.

2. Blockchain Fundamentals for Banking

Blockchain technology has transformative potential for the banking and financial sector. Its ability to provide transparency, security, and efficiency makes it an attractive option for various applications in banking.

Here's a breakdown of blockchain fundamentals and their implications for the banking industry:

1. Core Concepts of Blockchain

- **Blocks**:
    - **Definition**: A block is a data structure that contains a set of transactions. Each block includes a timestamp, a list of transactions, and a cryptographic hash of the previous block.

- o **Role in Banking**: Blocks ensure that transaction records are immutable and securely linked, which can enhance the integrity of financial records.
- **Chain**:
  - o **Definition**: Blocks are linked together in a sequential manner to form a chain. Each new block references the hash of the previous block, creating a continuous and unchangeable chain.
  - o **Role in Banking**: The chain structure ensures that records are tamper-proof, reducing the risk of fraud and errors in financial transactions.
- **Consensus Mechanisms**:
  - o **Definition**: Consensus mechanisms are protocols used to agree on the state of the blockchain. They ensure that all participants in the network have a consistent view of the data.
  - o **Role in Banking**: Consensus mechanisms, such as Proof of Work or Proof of Stake, help validate transactions and maintain trust without relying on a central authority.
- **Decentralization**:
  - o **Definition**: Blockchain is a decentralized network where no single entity has control over the entire ledger. Instead, multiple nodes (computers) participate in validating transactions and maintaining the blockchain.
  - o **Role in Banking**: Decentralization increases security and reduces the risk of single points of failure, making financial systems more resilient to attacks and outages.
- **Cryptographic Hashing**:
  - o **Definition**: Cryptographic hashing is the process of converting data into a fixed-size string of

characters, which appears random. Hashes are used to secure data and ensure its integrity.
    - **Role in Banking**: Hashing secures transaction data and prevents unauthorized alterations, enhancing the security of financial transactions and records.
- **Smart Contracts**:
    - **Definition**: Smart contracts are self-executing contracts with the terms of the agreement directly written into code. They automatically execute and enforce contract terms based on predefined conditions.
    - **Role in Banking**: Smart contracts automate and streamline various banking processes, such as loan approvals and settlements, reducing the need for intermediaries and minimizing errors.

2. Benefits of Blockchain in Banking

- **Increased Transparency**:
    - **Explanation**: Blockchain provides a transparent ledger that allows all participants to view and verify transactions. This transparency reduces the likelihood of fraud and enhances trust among parties.
    - **Example**: Transaction histories in trade finance can be transparently tracked and verified, reducing disputes and enhancing confidence among trading partners.
- **Enhanced Security**:
    - **Explanation**: The cryptographic nature of blockchain ensures that data is secure and tamper-proof. Decentralization also reduces the risk of single points of failure.

- o **Example**: Secure and tamper-proof record-keeping in cross-border payments protects against fraud and unauthorized access.
- **Reduced Costs**:
  - o **Explanation**: By eliminating intermediaries and automating processes, blockchain can significantly reduce transaction costs and operational expenses.
  - o **Example**: Blockchain can streamline and automate compliance and reporting processes, reducing administrative costs in banking operations.
- **Faster Transactions**:
  - o **Explanation**: Blockchain can speed up transaction processing by reducing the need for intermediaries and enabling real-time settlement.
  - o **Example**: Cross-border payments can be processed in minutes rather than days, improving efficiency for both banks and customers.
- **Improved Compliance and Auditability**:
  - o **Explanation**: The immutability and transparency of blockchain make it easier to track and audit transactions, enhancing compliance with regulatory requirements.
  - o **Example**: Blockchain can provide an immutable audit trail for regulatory reporting, simplifying compliance with anti-money laundering (AML) and know your customer (KYC) regulations.

3. **Real-World Examples in Banking**

1. **JPMorgan Chase's JPM Coin**:
   - o **Description**: JPMorgan Chase developed JPM Coin, a digital currency that uses blockchain technology to facilitate instantaneous and

secure transfers of funds between institutional clients.
- Impact: Enhances the efficiency of cross-border payments and reduces settlement times from days to seconds.

2. **Deutsche Bank's Digital Asset Custody:**
   - Description: Deutsche Bank is exploring blockchain for secure custody and management of digital assets. The platform aims to streamline the storage and transfer of digital securities.
   - Impact: Improves the security and efficiency of managing digital assets, providing a more secure solution for institutional investors.

3. **Santander's One Pay FX:**
   - Description: Santander launched One Pay FX, a blockchain-based app for international money transfers. It uses Ripple's blockchain technology to provide faster and more transparent cross-border payments.
   - Impact: Reduces the time and cost associated with international transfers, offering a competitive advantage in the remittance market.

4. **HSBC's Trade Finance Platform:**
   - Description: HSBC uses blockchain to enhance its trade finance operations through the Voltron platform. This platform digitizes and automates the trade finance process, including letters of credit and bills of lading.
   - Impact: Simplifies and accelerates the trade finance process, reducing paperwork and improving efficiency for global trade transactions.

5. **UBS and the Utility Settlement Coin (USC):**
    - **Description:** UBS is involved in the development of the Utility Settlement Coin, a blockchain-based digital currency designed for use in financial transactions and settlement processes.
    - **Impact:** Aims to improve settlement speed and efficiency while providing a secure and reliable digital currency solution for financial institutions.

Summary

Blockchain provides several advantages for the banking industry, including increased transparency, enhanced security, reduced costs, faster transactions, and improved compliance. Its decentralized, cryptographic, and immutable nature addresses many of the challenges faced by traditional financial systems. Real-world implementations by major banks illustrate how blockchain can transform various aspects of banking, from cross-border payments to trade finance, offering significant benefits in efficiency and security.

2.1 Decentralization Explained: *How decentralization impacts traditional banking systems*

Decentralization refers to the distribution of authority, control, and decision-making from a central entity to a distributed network. In the context of blockchain technology and banking, decentralization implies moving away from a centralized model, where a single institution or authority manages transactions and records, towards a distributed network where multiple participants collectively manage and validate these processes.

Here's a detailed explanation of how decentralization impacts traditional banking systems:

1. Elimination of Central Authorities

- **Traditional Banking Systems**:
    - Centralized banks and financial institutions act as intermediaries for transactions, maintain records, and oversee the entire financial process. They have the authority to process transactions, manage accounts, and enforce regulations.
- **Decentralized Systems**:
    - In a decentralized system, control is distributed across a network of nodes (computers) rather than being held by a central authority. This eliminates the need for intermediaries, as transactions are validated and recorded by the network participants themselves.
- **Impact**:
    - **Reduced Single Points of Failure**: With no central authority, the risk of failure or fraud is spread across the network, making the system more resilient.
    - **Increased Transparency**: Decentralization promotes transparency as transactions are visible

and verifiable by all network participants, reducing the likelihood of corruption or fraud.

2. Enhanced Security

- **Traditional Banking Systems**:
    - Security in centralized systems relies heavily on the integrity and protection of central databases. If these databases are compromised, the entire system is at risk.
- **Decentralized Systems**:
    - Decentralized networks use cryptographic techniques to secure data. Each participant in the network validates transactions, and data is stored across multiple nodes, making it more difficult for malicious actors to alter records or launch successful attacks.
- **Impact**:
    - **Increased Security**: The distributed nature of decentralized systems reduces the risk of data breaches and unauthorized access since there is no single point of vulnerability.
    - **Immutable Records**: Once recorded, transactions on a blockchain cannot be easily altered or deleted, providing a robust mechanism for maintaining data integrity.

3. Improved Efficiency and Speed

- **Traditional Banking Systems**:
    - Transactions often require intermediaries, such as clearinghouses and settlement institutions, which can introduce delays and additional costs. Cross-border payments, in particular, can take several days to process due to multiple intermediaries and time zone differences.
- **Decentralized Systems**:

- o Decentralized systems, such as blockchain networks, enable direct peer-to-peer transactions without intermediaries. Transactions are processed in real-time or near real-time, and smart contracts can automate and expedite various processes.
- **Impact**:
    - o **Faster Transactions**: Eliminating intermediaries speeds up transaction processing and reduces settlement times, making financial transactions more efficient.
    - o **Cost Reduction**: Reduced reliance on intermediaries lowers transaction costs and administrative fees, benefiting both financial institutions and their customers.

4. Increased Financial Inclusion
- **Traditional Banking Systems**:
    - o Access to financial services is often restricted by geographical location, regulatory requirements, and the need for physical infrastructure. This can exclude unbanked or underbanked populations from participating in the financial system.
- **Decentralized Systems**:
    - o Decentralized financial systems (DeFi) provide access to financial services through digital platforms, which can be accessed from anywhere with an internet connection. These platforms often require minimal documentation and offer services like lending, borrowing, and trading without traditional barriers.
- **Impact**:
    - o **Broader Access**: Decentralization helps increase financial inclusion by providing access to financial services for individuals who may not have access to traditional banking facilities.

- **Reduced Barriers**: Lower entry barriers and reduced reliance on physical infrastructure make it easier for underserved populations to participate in the global financial system.

5. Regulatory and Compliance Challenges

- **Traditional Banking Systems**:
  - Centralized banks are subject to strict regulatory oversight and compliance requirements, which help ensure the stability and integrity of the financial system. These regulations are enforced by central authorities and regulatory bodies.
- **Decentralized Systems**:
  - Decentralized systems operate without a central authority, which poses challenges for regulation and compliance. Ensuring adherence to regulatory requirements, such as anti-money laundering (AML) and know-your-customer (KYC) standards, becomes more complex.
- **Impact**:
  - **Regulatory Uncertainty**: The lack of central control can lead to regulatory uncertainties and difficulties in enforcing compliance, which may impact the adoption and integration of decentralized systems in traditional financial markets.
  - **Innovation vs. Regulation**: Balancing innovation with regulatory requirements is a challenge, as regulators work to adapt existing frameworks to accommodate the unique characteristics of decentralized technologies.

Real-World Examples of Decentralization in Banking

1. **Ripple (XRP)**:
   - **Description**: Ripple is a decentralized digital payment protocol that enables fast, low-cost

international transactions. It uses a consensus ledger rather than a traditional blockchain.
- **Impact**: Ripple's decentralized network improves the efficiency of cross-border payments and reduces costs associated with traditional intermediaries.

2. **Ethereum**:
   - **Description**: Ethereum is a decentralized platform that supports smart contracts and decentralized applications (DApps). It operates on a blockchain that allows for programmable transactions and automated agreements.
   - **Impact**: Ethereum's smart contract functionality enables financial services automation, reducing the need for intermediaries and enhancing operational efficiency.

3. **Bitcoin**:
   - **Description**: Bitcoin is a decentralized digital currency that operates on a peer-to-peer network. It eliminates the need for central banks and traditional financial intermediaries.
   - **Impact**: Bitcoin offers a decentralized alternative to traditional currencies, enabling secure, borderless transactions and promoting financial independence.

4. **Compound**:
   - **Description**: Compound is a decentralized lending and borrowing platform built on the Ethereum blockchain. It allows users to lend and borrow cryptocurrencies without relying on traditional financial institutions.
   - **Impact**: Compound's decentralized model provides access to financial services without

intermediaries, offering greater financial inclusion and efficiency.

5. **Ripple (XRP)**:
    - **Description**: Ripple is a decentralized digital payment protocol that enables fast, low-cost international transactions. It uses a consensus ledger rather than a traditional blockchain.
    - **Impact**: Ripple's decentralized network improves the efficiency of cross-border payments and reduces costs associated with traditional intermediaries.

6. **Ethereum**:
    - **Description**: Ethereum is a decentralized platform that supports smart contracts and decentralized applications (DApps). It operates on a blockchain that allows for programmable transactions and automated agreements.
    - **Impact**: Ethereum's smart contract functionality enables financial services automation, reducing the need for intermediaries and enhancing operational efficiency.

7. **Bitcoin**:
    - **Description**: Bitcoin is a decentralized digital currency that operates on a peer-to-peer network. It eliminates the need for central banks and traditional financial intermediaries.
    - **Impact**: Bitcoin offers a decentralized alternative to traditional currencies, enabling secure, borderless transactions and promoting financial independence.

8. **Compound**:
    - **Description**: Compound is a decentralized lending and borrowing platform built on the

> Ethereum blockchain. It allows users to lend and borrow cryptocurrencies without relying on traditional financial institutions.
>
> o **Impact**: Compound's decentralized model provides access to financial services without intermediaries, offering greater financial inclusion and efficiency.

Summary

Decentralization in banking fundamentally changes how financial systems operate by distributing control, increasing security, improving efficiency, and expanding access. It challenges traditional banking models by removing intermediaries, accelerating transactions, and enhancing transparency. While it offers significant benefits, such as reduced costs and increased financial inclusion, it also presents regulatory and compliance challenges that must be addressed to fully realize its potential. Real-world examples like Ripple, Ethereum, Bitcoin, and Compound illustrate how decentralization is transforming the banking and financial landscape.

2.2 Blockchain's Role in Banking: *The potential applications of blockchain technology in banking services*

Blockchain technology offers a range of transformative potential applications within the banking sector. By leveraging its decentralized, transparent, and secure nature, blockchain can significantly enhance various banking services. Here's a detailed look at how blockchain can be applied to banking services:

1. Cross-Border Payments and Remittances

- **Traditional Process**: Cross-border payments typically involve multiple intermediaries, including correspondent banks and clearinghouses. This process can be slow, costly, and subject to various fees and exchange rate fluctuations.
- **Blockchain Application**: Blockchain facilitates direct, peer-to-peer transactions between parties across borders. By using blockchain-based platforms like Ripple or Stellar, banks can streamline international payments, reduce transaction costs, and speed up the settlement process.
- **Example**: **Ripple** – Ripple's blockchain network allows banks and financial institutions to execute international transactions quickly and at a lower cost by bypassing traditional intermediaries.

2. Fraud Prevention and Security

- **Traditional Process**: Fraud detection in traditional banking systems relies on centralized databases and fraud detection systems, which can be vulnerable to breaches and tampering.
- **Blockchain Application**: Blockchain provides a decentralized ledger that is immutable and transparent. This means that once a transaction is recorded, it cannot be altered, reducing the risk of fraud and tampering. Banks can use blockchain to enhance the security of transaction records and reduce fraudulent activities.

- **Example**: **Chainalysis** – Chainalysis uses blockchain technology to track cryptocurrency transactions and detect suspicious activities, helping financial institutions combat fraud and money laundering.

3. *Smart Contracts*
   - **Traditional Process**: Traditional contracts often require intermediaries, such as lawyers or notaries, to enforce and manage agreements. This can lead to delays and increased costs.
   - **Blockchain Application**: Smart contracts are self-executing contracts with the terms of the agreement directly written into code. These contracts automatically execute and enforce terms when predefined conditions are met. Banks can use smart contracts for various purposes, including automating loan disbursements, trade finance, and compliance checks.
   - **Example**: **Synthetix** – Synthetix is a decentralized platform that uses smart contracts to enable the creation and trading of synthetic assets, which can be applied to various financial services, including derivatives and decentralized trading.

4. *Trade Finance*
   - **Traditional Process**: Trade finance involves multiple parties, including exporters, importers, banks, and insurance providers. The process can be complex, with extensive paperwork and manual verification.
   - **Blockchain Application**: Blockchain can digitize and automate trade finance processes by providing a single, immutable record of transactions. This reduces paperwork, speeds up the verification process, and enhances transparency. Blockchain-based platforms can streamline trade finance by enabling secure and transparent documentation and payment processes.
   - **Example**: **Marco Polo Network** – The Marco Polo Network uses blockchain technology to streamline trade

finance processes by providing a decentralized platform for managing trade documents and transactions.

5. KYC and AML Compliance

- **Traditional Process**: Know Your Customer (KYC) and Anti-Money Laundering (AML) compliance involve extensive data collection and verification processes. Banks often rely on manual processes and siloed data, leading to inefficiencies and high costs.
- **Blockchain Application**: Blockchain can improve KYC and AML processes by providing a decentralized and immutable record of customer identities and transactions. Banks can use blockchain to create a shared, tamper-proof repository of KYC information that can be accessed by multiple institutions, reducing duplication of efforts and improving compliance.
- **Example**: **Civic** – Civic uses blockchain technology to provide a decentralized identity verification platform that helps banks streamline KYC processes and enhance customer verification while maintaining privacy and security.

6. Securities Settlement and Clearing

- **Traditional Process**: The settlement and clearing of securities transactions involve multiple intermediaries, including clearinghouses and custodians. This process can be time-consuming and prone to errors.
- **Blockchain Application**: Blockchain can streamline securities settlement and clearing by providing a real-time, immutable ledger of transactions. This reduces the need for intermediaries and accelerates the settlement process. Blockchain-based platforms can facilitate instant settlement and reduce operational risks associated with traditional clearing systems.
- **Example**: **DTCC** – The Depository Trust & Clearing Corporation (DTCC) is exploring blockchain technology to enhance the efficiency and security of securities

settlement and clearing processes, aiming to reduce settlement times and operational risks.

7. Digital Identity Management

- **Traditional Process**: Digital identity management in traditional banking systems often relies on centralized databases and manual verification processes, which can be cumbersome and prone to identity theft.
- **Blockchain Application**: Blockchain provides a decentralized and secure way to manage digital identities. It allows individuals to control their personal data and share it selectively with institutions. Banks can use blockchain for secure and efficient digital identity verification and authentication.
- **Example**: **SelfKey** – SelfKey is a blockchain-based digital identity platform that allows individuals to manage and share their identity information securely with financial institutions and other service providers.

8. Lending and Borrowing

- **Traditional Process**: Traditional lending and borrowing processes involve intermediaries such as banks and credit agencies. These processes can be slow and involve significant paperwork and administrative costs.
- **Blockchain Application**: Blockchain-based lending platforms enable peer-to-peer lending and borrowing without traditional intermediaries. Smart contracts can automate the terms of loans, and decentralized platforms can facilitate direct lending and borrowing transactions.
- **Example**: **Compound** – Compound is a decentralized lending and borrowing platform that operates on the Ethereum blockchain, allowing users to lend and borrow cryptocurrencies directly without traditional financial intermediaries.

Summary

Blockchain technology offers transformative potential for the banking sector by addressing inefficiencies, enhancing security, and reducing costs across various processes. Its applications include streamlining cross-border payments, preventing fraud, automating contracts, improving trade finance, and enhancing KYC/AML compliance. Real-world examples like Ripple, Chainalysis, Synthetix, Marco Polo Network, Civic, DTCC, SelfKey, and Compound illustrate the diverse ways in which blockchain is reshaping banking services. By leveraging its decentralized and immutable nature, blockchain can drive innovation and efficiency in the financial industry.

2.3 Basic Terminology: *Key blockchain terms and concepts relevant to banking professionals*

Understanding blockchain terminology is crucial for banking professionals as the technology continues to integrate into financial services. Here's a concise guide to the key terms and concepts:

1. Blockchain

- **Definition**: A distributed ledger technology that records transactions across a network of computers in a way that is secure, transparent, and immutable. Each block contains a list of transactions and is linked to the previous block, forming a chain.
- **Relevance**: In banking, blockchain can be used for secure transaction records, cross-border payments, and smart contracts.

2. Block

- **Definition**: A collection of data or transactions that are bundled together and added to the blockchain. Each block contains a timestamp, a reference to the previous block (hash), and a list of transactions.
- **Relevance**: Blocks are the fundamental units of data in blockchain, crucial for understanding how transaction data is structured and secured.

3. Chain

- **Definition**: The sequence of blocks linked together in chronological order. Each block contains a reference to the previous block, creating a continuous and unalterable chain of blocks.
- **Relevance**: The chain ensures data integrity and security by making it difficult to alter past transactions without changing subsequent blocks.

4. Consensus Mechanism

- **Definition**: The protocol used by blockchain networks to agree on the validity of transactions and the state of the ledger. Common mechanisms include Proof of Work (PoW), Proof of Stake (PoS), and Byzantine Fault Tolerance (BFT).
- **Relevance**: Consensus mechanisms are crucial for ensuring that all participants in a blockchain network agree on transaction validity, which is important for maintaining the accuracy and security of financial transactions.

5. Cryptography

- **Definition**: The use of encryption techniques to secure information and control access. In blockchain, cryptography is used to create secure transactions and maintain data integrity.
- **Relevance**: Cryptography underpins the security of blockchain transactions, ensuring that data is encrypted and protected from unauthorized access.

6. Hash Function

- **Definition**: A mathematical function that converts an input (or 'message') into a fixed-size string of bytes, typically a hash code. In blockchain, hash functions are used to secure block data and create unique identifiers.
- **Relevance**: Hash functions ensure that each block is securely linked to the previous one and that data integrity is maintained.

7. Smart Contract

- **Definition**: Self-executing contracts with the terms written directly into code. They automatically enforce and execute contract terms based on predefined conditions.
- **Relevance**: In banking, smart contracts can automate processes such as loan disbursements, trade settlements,

and compliance checks, reducing the need for intermediaries.

8. *Decentralization*
    - **Definition**: The distribution of authority and control away from a central point. In a decentralized blockchain network, no single entity has control over the entire system.
    - **Relevance**: Decentralization enhances security and reduces the risk of single points of failure, making transactions more resilient to fraud and system failures.

9. *Ledger*
    - **Definition**: A record-keeping system that tracks transactions. In blockchain, the ledger is distributed and synchronized across all participants in the network.
    - **Relevance**: The ledger provides a transparent and immutable record of all transactions, which is vital for ensuring accurate and secure financial operations.

10. *Node*
    - **Definition**: A computer that participates in the blockchain network by maintaining a copy of the blockchain and validating transactions.
    - **Relevance**: Nodes are essential for the operation of the blockchain network, as they contribute to the network's security and transaction verification process.

11. *Public Key Infrastructure (PKI)*
    - **Definition**: A framework for managing digital keys and certificates. PKI is used in blockchain to secure communications and transactions.
    - **Relevance**: PKI helps ensure that transactions are secure and that the identities of parties involved are verified.

12. Token

- **Definition**: A digital asset or unit of value created on a blockchain. Tokens can represent various assets or utilities and can be fungible (e.g., cryptocurrencies) or non-fungible (e.g., digital collectibles).
- **Relevance**: Tokens are used in various financial applications, including cryptocurrencies, digital assets, and decentralized finance (DeFi) solutions.

13. Fork

- **Definition**: A change in the blockchain protocol that results in a divergence in the blockchain's history. Forks can be hard (resulting in a split into two separate chains) or soft (backward-compatible changes).
- **Relevance**: Forks can affect the continuity and compatibility of blockchain networks, impacting financial transactions and systems built on blockchain technology.

14. Consensus Algorithm

- **Definition**: The algorithm used to achieve agreement on the state of the blockchain. Common algorithms include Proof of Work (PoW), Proof of Stake (PoS), and Delegated Proof of Stake (DPoS).
- **Relevance**: Consensus algorithms are critical for ensuring that transactions are validated and recorded accurately in the blockchain, affecting the reliability and efficiency of financial operations.

15. Distributed Ledger Technology (DLT)

- **Definition**: A decentralized database that is maintained across multiple nodes or locations. Blockchain is a type of DLT, but not all DLTs are blockchains.
- **Relevance**: DLTs, including blockchain, are used to create transparent and tamper-proof records, enhancing security and accountability in financial transactions.

Real-World Examples

1. **Ripple**: Uses blockchain technology for cross-border payments and remittances, improving transaction speed and reducing costs.

2. **Chainalysis**: Employs blockchain technology for tracking cryptocurrency transactions and detecting fraudulent activities.

3. **Civic**: Utilizes blockchain for secure digital identity verification, enhancing the KYC process for financial institutions.

4. **Smartlands**: Implements smart contracts on blockchain to streamline and automate the issuance and trading of real estate tokens.

5. **DTCC**: The Depository Trust & Clearing Corporation is exploring blockchain to improve the efficiency and security of securities settlement and clearing.

By understanding these key terms and their applications, banking professionals can better grasp the implications of blockchain technology and its potential to transform the financial services industry.

3. Blockchain for Secure Transactions

Blockchain technology provides a robust framework for securing transactions by leveraging its inherent characteristics of decentralization, immutability, and transparency.

In a blockchain network, transactions are recorded on a decentralized ledger that is distributed across multiple nodes (computers) within the network. This decentralization means that there is no single point of failure, reducing the risk of data manipulation or unauthorized access. Each transaction is encrypted and linked to the previous transaction through cryptographic hashes, creating a secure chain of blocks that cannot be altered retroactively without altering all subsequent blocks, which is computationally impractical.

The security of blockchain transactions is further enhanced by consensus mechanisms such as Proof of Work (PoW) or Proof of

Stake (PoS). These mechanisms require participants to agree on the validity of transactions before they are added to the blockchain, ensuring that only legitimate transactions are recorded. For example, in PoW, participants (miners) solve complex mathematical problems to validate transactions, while in PoS, validators are chosen based on the number of coins they hold and are willing to "stake" as collateral.

Additionally, blockchain technology provides transparency through its public ledger. All transactions are visible to network participants, which allows for real-time tracking and verification of transaction history. This transparency helps prevent fraud and unauthorized activities, as any discrepancies or malicious attempts to alter the ledger are easily detectable by the network.

Smart contracts, which are self-executing contracts with the terms written directly into code, also play a crucial role in securing transactions on the blockchain. These contracts automatically enforce and execute agreements based on predefined conditions, reducing the need for intermediaries and minimizing the risk of human error or manipulation.

Overall, blockchain technology enhances transaction security by combining encryption, decentralization, consensus mechanisms, and transparency, creating a secure, reliable, and tamper-resistant environment for conducting financial and other types of transactions.

Blockchain technology enhances the security of transactions through several key functions:

1. Decentralization

Blockchain operates on a decentralized network of computers, or nodes, that collectively maintain the ledger. This decentralization eliminates the need for a central authority, reducing the risk of single points of failure and tampering. Each node in the network holds a copy of the entire ledger, ensuring that the transaction data is distributed and not controlled by any single entity, which enhances the overall security and resilience of the system.

2. Cryptographic Encryption

Transactions on a blockchain are secured using advanced cryptographic techniques. Each transaction is encrypted and linked to the previous transaction through a cryptographic hash. This hash function creates a unique digital signature for each block, which ensures the integrity of the transaction data. Any attempt to alter a transaction would require recalculating and altering all subsequent blocks, which is computationally infeasible, thereby securing the data against tampering.

3. Consensus Mechanisms

Blockchain networks use consensus mechanisms to validate transactions and add them to the ledger. These mechanisms, such as Proof of Work (PoW) or Proof of Stake (PoS), require network participants to agree on the validity of transactions before they are recorded. Consensus mechanisms prevent unauthorized transactions and fraud by ensuring that only verified and agreed-upon transactions are included in the blockchain, thus maintaining the integrity of the data.

4. Immutability

Once a transaction is recorded on the blockchain, it becomes part of an immutable ledger. This immutability is achieved through the cryptographic linking of blocks, making it virtually impossible to alter or delete historical transaction data without altering all subsequent blocks. This permanence ensures that transaction records remain unchanged and tamper-proof, providing a secure and reliable history of all transactions.

5. Transparency and Auditability

Blockchain provides transparency through its public ledger, where all transactions are visible to network participants. This transparency allows for real-time tracking and auditing of transactions, which helps detect and prevent fraudulent activities. Since every participant can view and verify transactions, any discrepancies or unauthorized actions are quickly identified and addressed, enhancing the security and accountability of transactions.

6. Smart Contracts

Smart contracts are self-executing agreements with the terms directly written into code that automatically execute and enforce transaction conditions. These contracts are executed on the blockchain, ensuring that they are tamper-proof and trustworthy. Smart contracts reduce the need for intermediaries and manual processing, minimizing the risk of errors or manipulation. They ensure that transactions are completed only when predefined conditions are met, enhancing both security and efficiency in transactional processes.

These functions collectively contribute to the robustness and security of transactions conducted over blockchain networks, making blockchain a powerful tool for safeguarding digital transactions and reducing the risk of fraud and manipulation.

Real-world examples:

Here are few real-world examples that illustrate how blockchain enhances transaction security through its key functions:

1. **Cross-Border Payments**
   - **Example: RippleNet**
     - **Description:** RippleNet facilitates cross-border payments by allowing banks and financial institutions to process transactions securely and efficiently. By leveraging blockchain's decentralization, cryptographic encryption, and consensus mechanisms, RippleNet enables real-time transactions that are transparent and secure, reducing fraud risks and transaction costs. For instance, Santander uses RippleNet to streamline international transfers, ensuring secure and quick payment processing.

2. **Supply Chain Management**
   - **Example: IBM Food Trust**
     - **Description:** IBM Food Trust utilizes blockchain to enhance the transparency and security of food supply chains. Each

transaction related to food products—from farm to table—is recorded on the blockchain, allowing all participants to track and verify the product's journey. The immutability and transparency of blockchain help prevent fraud and ensure product integrity, significantly reducing the risk of contamination and improving consumer trust.

3. Healthcare Records Management

- **Example: MedRec**
    - **Description:** MedRec, developed by MIT, leverages blockchain to manage electronic medical records securely. Patients control their own health data, which is recorded on a decentralized ledger. The cryptographic encryption and immutability of blockchain ensure that records cannot be altered without authorization, thereby protecting sensitive information from tampering and enhancing privacy in healthcare transactions.

4. Digital Identity Verification

- **Example: SelfKey**
    - **Description:** SelfKey is a blockchain-based identity management system that allows individuals to control their personal information securely. By utilizing blockchain's decentralization and smart contracts, SelfKey provides a secure and efficient method for verifying identities. This reduces the risk of identity theft and fraud in financial transactions, as users can selectively share their verified data with institutions without compromising their privacy.

5. Real Estate Transactions

- **Example: Propy**

- **Description:** Propy uses blockchain technology to facilitate real estate transactions securely and transparently. By recording property deeds and transactions on a blockchain, Propy ensures that all information is immutable and easily auditable. This reduces the risk of fraud and disputes, as all parties can verify ownership and transaction history in real-time. The use of smart contracts automates the transaction process, enhancing efficiency and security in real estate deals.

Summary

These examples highlight the various applications of blockchain technology in enhancing transaction security across different sectors. By leveraging its key functions—decentralization, cryptographic encryption, consensus mechanisms, immutability, transparency, and smart contracts—blockchain significantly reduces the risks associated with fraud and manipulation in transactions, thereby building trust and efficiency in diverse industries.

3.1 How Blockchain Secures Transactions: *Mechanisms that ensure transaction security and integrity*

Blockchain technology offers a transformative approach to secure transactions, enhancing the integrity, transparency, and efficiency of financial operations. Here's a detailed look at how blockchain ensures secure transactions:

1. Immutable Ledger

- **Definition**: Once data is recorded in a blockchain, it cannot be altered or deleted. Each block contains a unique cryptographic hash of the previous block, creating a secure chain.
- **How It Works**: When a transaction is added to a block and subsequently confirmed, it is cryptographically linked to all previous transactions. This linkage makes it extremely difficult for malicious actors to alter transaction history without being detected.
- **Benefit**: This immutability ensures that transaction records are tamper-proof and provides a permanent audit trail, enhancing security and accountability.

2. Decentralization

- **Definition**: In a blockchain network, data is distributed across multiple nodes (computers) rather than being stored in a single central server.
- **How It Works**: Each node maintains a copy of the blockchain and participates in the consensus process to validate transactions. This decentralization means there is no single point of failure, reducing the risk of attacks and data breaches.
- **Benefit**: Increased resilience to hacking and fraud, as attackers would need to compromise a majority of nodes to alter the blockchain.

3. Cryptographic Security
- **Definition**: Blockchain uses advanced cryptographic techniques to secure data and transactions.
- **How It Works**: Each transaction is encrypted using cryptographic algorithms, and public and private keys are used to verify the identities of the participants. Digital signatures ensure that transactions are authorized and have not been tampered with.
- **Benefit**: Ensures that only authorized parties can access or alter data, and that transactions are verifiable and secure.

4. Consensus Mechanisms
- **Definition**: Protocols used by blockchain networks to achieve agreement on the state of the ledger and validate transactions.
- **How It Works**: Common consensus mechanisms include Proof of Work (PoW), Proof of Stake (PoS), and Delegated Proof of Stake (DPoS). These mechanisms involve participants (nodes) agreeing on the validity of transactions based on predefined rules.
- **Benefit**: Ensures that all participants agree on the transaction data, reducing the risk of fraud and errors.

5. Smart Contracts
- **Definition**: Self-executing contracts with the terms written directly into code that automatically enforce and execute contractual agreements.
- **How It Works**: Smart contracts are deployed on the blockchain and execute automatically when predefined conditions are met. They facilitate, verify, or enforce the performance of contractual agreements without intermediaries.
- **Benefit**: Reduces the risk of human error and fraud, and speeds up transaction processes by automating contract execution.

6. Transparency

- **Definition**: All transactions recorded on a blockchain are visible to participants in the network.
- **How It Works**: Each transaction is stored in a block and is accessible to all nodes within the network. This transparency allows participants to view and verify transactions.
- **Benefit**: Enhances trust and accountability, as all actions are recorded and visible, making it easier to track and audit transactions.

7. Access Control

- **Definition**: Mechanisms that ensure only authorized users can access or perform specific actions on the blockchain.
- **How It Works**: Access control is enforced through cryptographic keys and permissions. Participants use private keys to sign transactions and authenticate their identities.
- **Benefit**: Ensures that only authorized individuals can initiate or approve transactions, enhancing security.

Real-World Examples

1. **JPMorgan Chase**:
   - **Application**: JPMorgan Chase has developed its own blockchain platform called JPM Coin, designed for secure and efficient transactions between institutional clients. This platform leverages blockchain to enable real-time settlement and secure transfers of value.

2. **Deutsche Bank**:
   - **Application**: Deutsche Bank is exploring blockchain for improving trade finance processes. By using blockchain, the bank aims to streamline and secure transactions, reduce

> fraud, and improve transparency in supply chain finance.
>
> 3. **Visa**:
>   o **Application**: Visa is incorporating blockchain technology into its payment systems to enhance security and speed. Their blockchain-based solutions aim to reduce transaction costs and fraud while increasing transaction speed.
>
> 4. **IBM and Maersk**:
>   o **Application**: IBM and Maersk have developed TradeLens, a blockchain-based platform for global trade that enhances the security and transparency of shipping transactions. It allows all participants in the supply chain to track and verify shipments in real time.
>
> 5. **Circle**:
>   o **Application**: Circle uses blockchain for its digital currency platform, USDC, which provides secure and transparent transactions. By leveraging blockchain, Circle ensures that digital dollar transactions are traceable, verifiable, and tamper-proof.

By implementing blockchain technology, financial institutions can significantly enhance transaction security, improve transparency, and reduce the risk of fraud. The technology's key features, including immutability, decentralization, and cryptographic security, make it a powerful tool for modernizing financial operations and ensuring secure transactions.

3.2 Cryptographic Principles: *Introduction to cryptography techniques used in blockchain for securing data*

Cryptography is fundamental to blockchain technology, providing the mechanisms that ensure data security, integrity, and privacy. Here's an introduction to key cryptographic techniques used in blockchain:

1. Hash Functions

- **Definition**: Hash functions are algorithms that take an input (or message) and produce a fixed-size string of bytes, typically a hash value. The output is unique to each unique input.
- **How It Works**: In blockchain, hash functions create a unique fingerprint for each block's data. When a block is created, its contents are processed by a hash function to produce a hash value. Any change in the block's data would result in a completely different hash value, thus ensuring data integrity.
- **Common Algorithms**: SHA-256 (used in Bitcoin) and Keccak-256 (used in Ethereum).
- **Benefit**: Ensures data integrity by making it virtually impossible to alter data without changing the hash value, thus alerting the network to tampering.

2. Digital Signatures

- **Definition**: Digital signatures are cryptographic techniques that authenticate the identity of the sender and ensure the integrity of the message.
- **How It Works**: A digital signature is created using a private key to sign a transaction or block. The corresponding public key is used to verify the signature. This proves that the transaction was created by the owner of the private key and that it has not been altered.

- **Common Algorithms**: RSA, ECDSA (Elliptic Curve Digital Signature Algorithm).
- **Benefit**: Provides authentication and non-repudiation, ensuring that transactions are legitimate and traceable back to the sender.

3. Public and Private Key Cryptography

- **Definition**: A cryptographic system that uses pairs of keys—public keys and private keys—to secure data.
- **How It Works**:
    - **Public Key**: Shared openly and used to encrypt data or verify a digital signature.
    - **Private Key**: Kept secret and used to decrypt data or create a digital signature.
- **Application in Blockchain**: Users have a public key (address) where others can send cryptocurrency, and a private key to access and control their assets.
- **Benefit**: Ensures secure transactions and user privacy. Only the holder of the private key can access their assets or sign transactions.

4. Merkle Trees

- **Definition**: A Merkle tree is a binary tree in which each leaf node is a hash of a block of data, and each non-leaf node is a hash of its child nodes.
- **How It Works**: Merkle trees efficiently summarize and verify the integrity of large sets of data. In a blockchain, Merkle trees are used to aggregate transactions into a single hash that represents all the transactions in a block.
- **Benefit**: Allows efficient and secure verification of large data sets, as only the root hash needs to be checked to ensure the integrity of all transactions in a block.

5. Consensus Algorithms

- **Definition**: Algorithms used to achieve agreement among distributed nodes in a blockchain network on the validity of transactions and blocks.
- **Common Algorithms**:
    o **Proof of Work (PoW)**: Requires miners to solve complex mathematical problems to validate transactions and create new blocks. Used in Bitcoin.
    o **Proof of Stake (PoS)**: Validators are chosen based on the number of coins they hold and are willing to "stake" as collateral. Used in Ethereum 2.0.
    o **Delegated Proof of Stake (DPoS)**: Stakeholders elect delegates who validate transactions and create blocks. Used in EOS.
- **Benefit**: Ensures that all nodes in a decentralized network agree on the state of the blockchain, maintaining consistency and preventing double-spending.

6. Zero-Knowledge Proofs

- **Definition**: Cryptographic methods that allow one party to prove to another party that a statement is true without revealing any additional information.
- **How It Works**: The prover demonstrates knowledge of a fact or solution without actually disclosing the fact itself. For example, proving you have the right credentials without revealing them.
- **Application in Blockchain**: Used in privacy-focused cryptocurrencies like Zcash to enhance transaction privacy.
- **Benefit**: Protects user privacy and confidentiality while still proving the validity of a transaction.

Real-World Examples

1. **Bitcoin**:
   - **Hash Function**: Uses SHA-256 for creating hashes of transaction data and blocks.
   - **Digital Signatures**: Utilizes ECDSA for securing transactions and verifying user identities.
2. **Ethereum**:
   - **Hash Function**: Employs Keccak-256 for block and transaction hashing.
   - **Smart Contracts**: Uses public and private key cryptography to manage and execute smart contracts securely.
3. **Zcash**:
   - **Zero-Knowledge Proofs**: Implements zk-SNARKs (Zero-Knowledge Succinct Non-Interactive Arguments of Knowledge) to provide transaction privacy.
4. **Ripple**:
   - **Consensus Algorithm**: Uses the Ripple Protocol Consensus Algorithm (RPCA) to achieve consensus without mining, allowing for fast and secure transactions.
5. **Chainlink**:
   - **Oracles**: Uses cryptographic techniques to securely fetch and verify off-chain data for use in smart contracts, enhancing the reliability and security of decentralized applications.

By leveraging these cryptographic principles, blockchain technology ensures secure, transparent, and tamper-proof transactions, fundamentally transforming the way data and value are managed in digital systems.

4. Smart Contracts and Their Applications

Smart contracts, an innovative feature of blockchain technology, are self-executing agreements with the terms of the contract directly written into code. They automatically execute, control, and document legally relevant events and actions according to the terms of the agreement.

Here's how smart contracts are transforming banking and finance:

1. Automation of Transactions

Smart contracts automate complex financial transactions by executing predefined actions when specific conditions are met. For instance, in trade finance, smart contracts can automatically release payments upon the verification of shipment documents, eliminating the need for intermediaries. This automation speeds up transaction processing, reduces manual errors, and enhances operational efficiency.

2. Improved Compliance and Risk Management

Smart contracts ensure that all parties adhere to the terms of an agreement by automatically enforcing compliance rules. In the context of regulatory requirements, they can be programmed to automatically apply rules related to anti-money laundering (AML) and know your customer (KYC) regulations. This reduces the risk of non-compliance and improves the accuracy of regulatory reporting by ensuring that only compliant transactions are processed.

3. Enhanced Transparency and Trust

Smart contracts are stored on a blockchain, providing a transparent and immutable record of all transactions. This transparency helps in building trust among parties, as all participants can access and verify the contract's terms and execution history. For example, in syndicated loans, smart contracts can provide all lenders with real-time updates on the loan's status, ensuring transparency and reducing disputes.

4. Efficient Derivatives and Financial Instruments

In the derivatives market, smart contracts facilitate the creation and management of financial instruments such as options and futures. These contracts can automatically calculate and execute payments based on market conditions, reducing the need for manual intervention and minimizing the risk of errors. By automating the settlement process, smart contracts can improve the efficiency and accuracy of financial derivatives trading.

5. Streamlined Loan Processing and Management

Smart contracts can revolutionize the loan industry by automating the entire loan lifecycle. From approval to disbursement and repayment, smart contracts can handle all aspects of loan processing. For example, they can automatically release loan funds once all conditions are met and track payments to ensure timely repayment. This reduces administrative costs and processing times, enhancing the overall efficiency of lending operations.

6. Enhanced Asset Management

Smart contracts facilitate efficient and transparent asset management by automating the transfer and tracking of ownership. In investment management, smart contracts can handle the issuance and redemption of investment funds, track asset performance, and execute trades based on predefined criteria. This automation streamlines asset management processes and provides real-time updates, improving the accuracy and efficiency of managing investments.

7. Fraud Prevention and Security

By ensuring that contracts are executed exactly as programmed and providing a secure, tamper-proof record of transactions, smart contracts help prevent fraud and unauthorized modifications. In financial services, this reduces the likelihood of fraudulent activities and enhances the security of transactions. For instance, in cross-border payments, smart contracts can verify and authenticate transactions before execution, minimizing the risk of fraud.

In summary, smart contracts are revolutionizing banking and finance by automating transactions, improving compliance, enhancing transparency, and increasing efficiency. Their ability to execute and enforce contract terms automatically offers significant benefits, including cost savings, reduced errors, and improved trust among parties. As adoption of blockchain technology grows, smart contracts are expected to play an increasingly central role in transforming financial services.

Here are a few real-world examples illustrating how smart contracts are applied in banking and finance:

1. Automation of Transactions

Example: De Beers and Everledger

De Beers, a leading diamond company, uses blockchain technology to track the provenance of diamonds. Smart contracts are employed to automate and verify transactions related to the diamond's journey from mine to market. When a diamond is sold, a smart contract executes the payment and updates the blockchain with the new ownership information. This automation reduces the need for intermediaries and ensures that each transaction is transparent and traceable.

2. Improved Compliance and Risk Management

Example: U.S. Federal Reserve's Digital Dollar Project

In exploring digital currency solutions, the Federal Reserve is considering the use of smart contracts to enhance regulatory compliance and risk management. Smart contracts could automate compliance checks, such as verifying transaction limits and performing anti-money laundering (AML) checks. This approach would streamline regulatory processes and improve the accuracy of compliance monitoring, while reducing manual intervention and potential errors.

3. Enhanced Transparency and Trust

Example: Syndicated Loans via Finastra's Fusion LenderComm

Finastra's Fusion LenderComm platform uses blockchain and smart contracts to manage syndicated loans. Smart contracts automate the process of loan servicing and provide real-time updates to all participating lenders. This transparency helps in reducing disputes and building trust among lenders, as everyone has access to the same information regarding the loan's status and payments.

4. Efficient Derivatives and Financial Instruments

Example: DTCC's Blockchain-Based Derivatives Clearing

The Depository Trust & Clearing Corporation (DTCC) has been exploring blockchain technology for clearing and settling derivatives. By using smart contracts, DTCC aims to automate the settlement process for derivatives contracts. Smart contracts calculate and execute payments based on market conditions, streamlining operations and reducing the potential for errors and delays in derivatives trading.

5. Streamlined Loan Processing and Management

Example: Figure Technologies' Home Equity Lines of Credit (HELOCs)

Figure Technologies uses blockchain and smart contracts to streamline the processing and management of Home Equity Lines of Credit (HELOCs). The platform automates loan origination, disbursement, and repayment processes. Smart contracts ensure that funds are released only when all conditions are met and track repayments in real-time, significantly reducing administrative costs and processing times.

6. Enhanced Asset Management

Example: Swiss Digital Asset Platform - Crypto Finance AG

Crypto Finance AG in Switzerland uses blockchain and smart contracts to manage digital assets. The platform automates the issuance and redemption of investment funds, tracks asset performance, and executes trades based on predefined criteria set within smart contracts. This approach enhances the efficiency of asset management by providing real-time updates and reducing manual intervention.

7. Fraud Prevention and Security

Example: Circle's USDC Stablecoin

Circle, a major player in the cryptocurrency space, uses smart contracts for its USDC stablecoin. Smart contracts ensure that the issuance and redemption of USDC are transparent and secure. Transactions are verified and executed based on predetermined conditions, which reduces the risk of fraud and ensures the integrity of the stablecoin's value.

These examples demonstrate the practical applications of smart contracts in various facets of banking and finance. By automating processes, improving compliance, enhancing transparency, and increasing security, smart contracts are transforming traditional financial systems and setting new standards for efficiency and trust.

4.1 What Are Smart Contracts?: *Basic concept of smart contracts and how they work on blockchain platforms*

Smart contracts are self-executing contracts with the terms of the agreement directly written into code. They run on blockchain platforms and automatically enforce and execute the terms of a contract without the need for intermediaries. Here's a breakdown of their basic concept and functionality:

1. Basic Concept of Smart Contracts

- **Definition**: A smart contract is a computer program that automatically executes and manages the terms of a contract when predefined conditions are met. It operates on a blockchain, ensuring transparency and immutability.

- **Functionality**: Smart contracts are written in programming languages specific to blockchain platforms, such as Solidity for Ethereum. They are deployed onto the blockchain where they interact with other contracts, data, and external systems.

- **Automation**: Once the conditions coded into the smart contract are satisfied, the contract executes its terms automatically. This reduces the need for human intervention and can minimize errors or disputes.

- **Trust and Security**: The blockchain's decentralized nature ensures that once a smart contract is deployed, it cannot be altered, which provides security and builds trust among parties involved.

2. How Smart Contracts Work

1. **Creation**:
    - **Code Writing**: Developers write the contract's terms and logic using a blockchain-specific programming language.

- **Deployment**: The smart contract code is deployed to the blockchain network, making it immutable and distributed across all nodes.

2. **Execution**:
    - **Triggering**: Smart contracts are triggered by specific events or conditions encoded within them. These triggers could be financial transactions, data inputs, or interactions with other smart contracts.
    - **Processing**: When the conditions are met, the contract automatically executes the predefined actions. This could involve transferring assets, updating records, or sending notifications.

3. **Verification**:
    - **Consensus**: The blockchain network uses consensus algorithms to verify and validate the contract's execution. This ensures that the terms were executed correctly and transparently.

4. **Completion**:
    - **Immutable Record**: Once executed, the results of the smart contract are recorded on the blockchain, providing a permanent and verifiable record of the transaction or contract fulfillment.

3. Examples of Smart Contracts in Action

- **Financial Transactions**: In decentralized finance (DeFi), smart contracts facilitate automated lending and borrowing. For example, if a borrower provides collateral and meets the repayment conditions, the smart contract automatically releases the funds.
- **Supply Chain Management**: Smart contracts can be used to track goods as they move through the supply chain. For instance, a smart contract could automatically release payment to a supplier once the shipment is verified as delivered and accepted.

- **Insurance**: In the insurance industry, smart contracts can automate claim processing. If an insured event (e.g., flight delay) is verified through an oracle (a data feed), the contract can automatically trigger a payout to the policyholder.
- **Real Estate**: Smart contracts streamline property transactions by automating tasks like transferring ownership and managing escrow. Once the payment is made and all conditions are verified, the ownership title is transferred automatically.

4. Advantages of Smart Contracts

- **Efficiency**: Automates and speeds up contract execution, reducing delays and administrative overhead.
- **Cost-Effective**: Minimizes the need for intermediaries, lowering transaction costs.
- **Transparency**: Provides a clear, immutable record of all contract activities and transactions.
- **Security**: Enhanced security due to cryptographic encryption and decentralized nature of the blockchain.

5. Challenges and Considerations

- **Complexity**: Writing and deploying smart contracts requires technical expertise and thorough testing to avoid bugs or vulnerabilities.
- **Scalability**: Blockchain networks can face scalability issues that may impact the performance of smart contracts.
- **Legal and Regulatory**: The legal status of smart contracts varies by jurisdiction, and integrating them into traditional legal frameworks can be complex.

Real-World Examples

1. **Ethereum**:
    - **Platform**: Ethereum is the most prominent blockchain platform supporting smart

contracts, enabling a wide range of decentralized applications (dApps) and services.

2. **Chainlink**:
   - **Oracle Integration**: Chainlink provides decentralized oracles that feed real-world data to smart contracts, enabling them to interact with external systems and data sources securely.

3. **Uniswap**:
   - **Decentralized Exchange**: Uniswap utilizes smart contracts to facilitate the exchange of cryptocurrencies without the need for a centralized authority.

4. **Synthetix**:
   - **Synthetic Assets**: Synthetix allows the creation of synthetic assets using smart contracts, enabling users to trade various assets like cryptocurrencies, commodities, and stocks in a decentralized manner.

5. **Centrifuge**:
   - **Supply Chain Financing**: Centrifuge uses smart contracts to automate and manage supply chain financing, allowing businesses to tokenize and finance their invoices on the blockchain.

Smart contracts represent a significant advancement in how agreements and transactions can be managed, offering enhanced automation, security, and efficiency in various industries.

4.2 Benefits of Smart Contracts in Finance: *Advantages of using smart contracts in financial services*

Smart contracts offer numerous advantages to the financial services industry by automating and enhancing various aspects of financial transactions and operations. Here are some key benefits:

1. Increased Efficiency

- **Automation**: Smart contracts automatically execute transactions and enforce contractual terms when predefined conditions are met. This reduces the need for manual intervention and speeds up processes, such as loan approvals, payment settlements, and trade executions.
- **Streamlined Operations**: By automating routine tasks and reducing paperwork, smart contracts streamline financial operations, cutting down on processing times and administrative overhead.

2. Cost Reduction

- **Elimination of Intermediaries**: Traditional financial transactions often require intermediaries, such as brokers, notaries, and clearinghouses. Smart contracts eliminate the need for these intermediaries, reducing associated fees and transaction costs.
- **Reduced Errors**: Automated execution minimizes the risk of human errors and discrepancies, leading to more accurate and cost-effective transactions.

3. Enhanced Transparency

- **Immutable Records**: Transactions and contract executions are recorded on a blockchain, creating a transparent and tamper-proof record. This enhances accountability and allows all parties to verify the execution and terms of the contract.
- **Auditability**: The blockchain provides an auditable trail of all contract interactions and changes, improving

transparency and compliance with regulatory requirements.

4. Improved Security

- **Cryptographic Protection**: Smart contracts use cryptographic techniques to secure data and transactions. This ensures that the terms of the contract are protected against tampering and unauthorized access.
- **Decentralization**: By operating on a decentralized blockchain network, smart contracts are less vulnerable to single points of failure or attacks compared to centralized systems.

5. Greater Accuracy

- **Error Reduction**: Smart contracts execute automatically based on coded logic, reducing the risk of manual errors and discrepancies in financial transactions.
- **Consistent Execution**: The predefined conditions are executed exactly as programmed, ensuring consistent and predictable outcomes.

6. Faster Transactions

- **Real-Time Processing**: Smart contracts enable real-time processing of transactions and contract executions, significantly reducing delays and waiting times associated with traditional financial processes.
- **24/7 Availability**: Unlike traditional financial institutions with limited operating hours, smart contracts can execute transactions and enforce terms at any time, providing greater flexibility.

7. Enhanced Compliance and Risk Management

- **Regulatory Compliance**: Smart contracts can be programmed to comply with regulatory requirements, automatically enforcing rules and ensuring adherence to legal standards.

- **Risk Mitigation**: By automating contract execution and reducing manual intervention, smart contracts help mitigate risks associated with errors, fraud, and disputes.

8. Innovative Financial Products

- **Decentralized Finance (DeFi)**: Smart contracts enable the creation of decentralized financial products and services, such as automated lending platforms, decentralized exchanges, and synthetic assets, broadening the range of financial instruments available to users.
- **Tokenization**: Financial assets can be tokenized and managed through smart contracts, facilitating new forms of investment, ownership, and trading.

Real-World Examples

1. **DeFi Platforms (e.g., MakerDAO)**:
    - **Function**: MakerDAO uses smart contracts to provide decentralized lending and stablecoin issuance. Users can collateralize their assets to take out loans in the form of DAI, a stablecoin.
2. **Ethereum**:
    - **Function**: Ethereum is a blockchain platform that supports a wide range of smart contracts, enabling decentralized applications (dApps) and services, including financial products like decentralized exchanges and lending platforms.
3. **Chainlink**:
    - **Function**: Chainlink provides decentralized oracles that connect smart contracts with real-world data, enabling applications such as automated insurance payouts based on weather data or market prices.
4. **Uniswap**:

- o **Function**: Uniswap is a decentralized exchange that uses smart contracts to facilitate the trading of cryptocurrencies without the need for a central authority or intermediary.

5. **Synthetix**:
    - o **Function**: Synthetix uses smart contracts to enable the creation and trading of synthetic assets that mimic the value of real-world assets like stocks, commodities, and currencies.

6. **Centrifuge**:
    - o **Function**: Centrifuge uses smart contracts for supply chain financing, allowing businesses to tokenize and finance their invoices through blockchain-based smart contracts.

Smart contracts are transforming the financial services industry by enhancing efficiency, reducing costs, improving transparency and security, and enabling innovative financial products. Their ability to automate and streamline processes makes them a powerful tool for modernizing financial operations.

5. Blockchain in Payments and Transfers

Blockchain technology is significantly reshaping the landscape of payments and transfers, offering transformative benefits in terms of speed, cost, security, and transparency.

Here's an overview of how blockchain is impacting these financial processes:

1. Faster Transactions

Blockchain enables near-instantaneous processing of payments and transfers compared to traditional banking systems. In traditional financial networks, cross-border payments can take several days due to the involvement of multiple intermediaries, currency conversions, and manual processing. Blockchain technology, with its decentralized nature and direct peer-to-peer transactions, reduces the time required to process payments from days to minutes or even seconds. For example, Ripple's XRP and

Stellar's XLM are blockchain-based platforms designed to facilitate rapid cross-border payments.

2. Lower Transaction Costs

By eliminating intermediaries and reducing the need for multiple financial institutions to process and validate transactions, blockchain technology significantly lowers transaction costs. Traditional payment systems often involve fees charged by banks and payment processors at each step of the transaction. Blockchain, with its decentralized and direct nature, reduces or even eliminates these fees. For instance, the use of Bitcoin for international money transfers can be more cost-effective compared to traditional wire transfers, as it bypasses intermediary banks and payment processors.

3. Increased Security

Blockchain enhances the security of payments and transfers through its cryptographic features and immutable ledger. Each transaction is encrypted and added to a chain of blocks that is distributed across multiple nodes. This makes it highly resistant to tampering and fraud. For example, in the case of cryptocurrencies like Bitcoin and Ethereum, transactions are secured by cryptographic algorithms and are verified by a consensus mechanism, making it extremely difficult for malicious actors to alter transaction data or double-spend coins.

4. Transparency and Traceability

Blockchain provides a transparent and immutable record of all transactions, which enhances traceability and accountability. Every transaction is recorded on a public ledger that can be accessed by network participants, allowing for real-time tracking and verification. This transparency is particularly valuable in sectors like supply chain management, where the provenance of funds and products can be tracked from origin to destination. For example, blockchain-based payment solutions can provide a clear audit trail for charitable donations, ensuring that funds are used as intended.

5. Decentralized Payments

Blockchain technology facilitates decentralized payments, allowing transactions to occur directly between parties without the need for a central authority. This decentralized approach reduces the risk of systemic failures and single points of control. For example, decentralized finance (DeFi) platforms like Uniswap and Aave enable users to conduct peer-to-peer transactions and access financial services without relying on traditional banks or intermediaries.

6. Cross-Border Transactions

Blockchain is particularly effective in streamlining cross-border transactions. Traditional international transfers often involve multiple banks, each with its own fees, processing times, and exchange rates. Blockchain-based solutions enable direct transactions between parties in different countries, reducing the complexity and cost associated with cross-border payments. For instance, the use of stablecoins, such as USD Coin (USDC) or Tether (USDT), facilitates stable and efficient cross-border transfers by maintaining a consistent value relative to fiat currencies.

7. Smart Contracts for Payment Automation

Smart contracts—self-executing contracts with the terms written into code—automate payment processes and enforce contractual agreements. In payment scenarios, smart contracts can automatically trigger payments when predefined conditions are met, reducing the need for manual intervention and minimizing the risk of errors. For example, in real estate transactions, a smart contract can automatically release funds to the seller once all conditions of the contract are fulfilled, such as the transfer of property title.

In summary, blockchain technology revolutionizes payments and transfers by offering faster processing times, lower transaction costs, enhanced security, greater transparency, and improved efficiency. Through decentralized and automated mechanisms, blockchain is transforming traditional financial processes and providing innovative solutions for modern payment needs.

Here are some real-world applications of blockchain technology in payments and transfers that illustrate its transformative impact:

1. Ripple (XRP) for Cross-Border Payments

Ripple provides a blockchain-based payment protocol designed to facilitate real-time, cross-border transactions. Unlike traditional methods that can take days and involve multiple intermediaries, Ripple's network allows for instant settlement of international payments, significantly reducing transaction times and fees. Ripple's technology is used by various financial institutions, including Santander and Standard Chartered, to streamline cross-border transactions and improve liquidity management.

2. Stellar (XLM) for International Transfers

Stellar is a blockchain platform designed to enhance cross-border payments and financial inclusion. Stellar's network allows for fast and low-cost transactions between different currencies, making it easier for individuals and businesses in developing regions to participate in the global economy. Companies like IBM have partnered with Stellar to develop solutions for international payments, such as IBM's World Wire, which aims to enable instant and low-cost transfers across borders.

3. Bitcoin for Peer-to-Peer Payments

Bitcoin, the first and most well-known cryptocurrency, enables peer-to-peer transactions without the need for intermediaries. Bitcoin's blockchain provides a secure and decentralized way to transfer funds globally. Platforms like BitPay and CoinGate allow merchants to accept Bitcoin payments, offering a low-cost alternative to traditional payment processing systems. Bitcoin's use in remittances is particularly notable, providing a cost-effective solution for individuals sending money across borders.

4. USDC and Tether (USDT) for Stablecoin Transactions

USD Coin (USDC) and **Tether (USDT)** are stablecoins pegged to the value of fiat currencies like the US Dollar. They are used for stable and efficient cross-border transfers, minimizing the volatility typically associated with cryptocurrencies. These stablecoins are integrated into various blockchain platforms and exchanges, enabling users to transfer value quickly and with minimal fees. For example, platforms like Circle and Coinbase use USDC for seamless transactions and trading.

5. DeFi Platforms like Uniswap for Decentralized Trading

Uniswap is a decentralized finance (DeFi) platform that facilitates automated, peer-to-peer trading of cryptocurrencies. Using smart contracts, Uniswap allows users to trade tokens directly on the blockchain without intermediaries. This decentralized approach reduces transaction fees and processing times while enhancing transparency. Uniswap's liquidity pools enable users to provide liquidity and earn rewards, further demonstrating the efficiency and innovation of blockchain-based financial services.

6. VeChain for Supply Chain Payments

VeChain utilizes blockchain technology to improve transparency and efficiency in supply chain management, including payments. By recording every step of a product's journey on the VeChain blockchain, businesses can ensure that payments are only made when certain conditions are met. This application is particularly useful in complex supply chains where timely and accurate payments are critical. For instance, VeChain's collaboration with companies like Walmart China helps streamline the payment process by ensuring that all supply chain activities are documented and verified.

7. Figure Technologies for Home Equity Lines of Credit (HELOCs)

Figure Technologies uses blockchain technology to automate and streamline the processing of Home Equity Lines of Credit (HELOCs). Smart contracts handle loan origination, disbursement, and repayment processes, reducing administrative costs and processing times. By using blockchain, Figure ensures that funds are released only when all conditions are met and tracks repayments in real-time, enhancing efficiency and security in the lending process.

These real-world applications demonstrate how blockchain technology is revolutionizing payments and transfers by offering faster processing, lower costs, enhanced security, and greater transparency. From international payments and peer-to-peer transfers to stablecoin transactions and decentralized trading, blockchain is driving significant improvements in financial services.

5.1 Blockchain for Payment Processing: *How blockchain technology improves payment processing efficiency*

Blockchain technology offers significant improvements to payment processing by addressing key inefficiencies and challenges traditionally faced in financial transactions. Here's how blockchain enhances payment processing efficiency:

1. Faster Transactions

- **Real-Time Settlement**: Traditional payment systems, especially cross-border transactions, can take several days to settle due to the involvement of multiple intermediaries and time zone differences. Blockchain technology enables near-instantaneous settlement of transactions by directly recording them on a decentralized ledger. This reduces processing times from days to minutes or even seconds.
- **24/7 Availability**: Unlike traditional financial institutions that operate within specific hours, blockchain networks are operational 24/7. This continuous operation allows for real-time payment processing at any time, regardless of business hours or weekends.

2. Cost Reduction

- **Elimination of Intermediaries**: Blockchain reduces the need for intermediaries, such as banks and payment processors, by allowing direct peer-to-peer transactions. This eliminates intermediary fees and reduces transaction costs.
- **Lower Transaction Fees**: By bypassing traditional banking infrastructure and using decentralized networks, blockchain transactions can significantly lower transaction fees, especially for international payments.

3. Enhanced Security

- **Cryptographic Protection**: Blockchain uses advanced cryptographic techniques to secure transactions. Each transaction is encrypted and recorded in a block that is linked to previous blocks, creating an immutable and tamper-proof ledger. This enhances the security of payment information and reduces the risk of fraud.
- **Decentralized Consensus**: Transactions on a blockchain are validated by a network of nodes through consensus mechanisms (e.g., Proof of Work, Proof of Stake). This decentralized approach reduces the risk of centralized points of failure and fraud.

4. Transparency and Traceability

- **Immutable Ledger**: Blockchain provides a transparent and immutable ledger of all transactions. Once a transaction is recorded, it cannot be altered or deleted, which ensures complete and accurate records. This transparency helps in tracking and verifying transactions easily.
- **Auditability**: The permanent and public ledger allows for real-time auditing and verification of transactions. This simplifies compliance and regulatory reporting by providing a clear trail of all payment activities.

5. Reduced Errors and Disputes

- **Automated Reconciliation**: Blockchain's automated and programmable nature reduces manual intervention and the potential for human errors. Smart contracts can automate payment terms and conditions, reducing discrepancies and disputes between parties.
- **Immutable Records**: Since transactions are recorded on an immutable ledger, it becomes easier to resolve disputes as there is a clear and unchangeable record of all transactions.

6. Cross-Border Payments

- **Efficient International Transactions**: Cross-border payments traditionally involve multiple banks and clearinghouses, leading to delays and higher costs. Blockchain simplifies cross-border transactions by enabling direct transfers between parties on a single decentralized network, reducing the time and costs associated with international payments.
- **Currency Conversion**: Blockchain can facilitate real-time currency conversion and settlement through the use of digital currencies or stablecoins, further enhancing the efficiency of cross-border transactions.

7. Innovation and Integration

- **Programmable Payments**: Blockchain allows for programmable payments through smart contracts, which can automatically execute transactions based on predefined conditions. This opens up possibilities for automated payment solutions and complex financial arrangements.
- **Integration with Emerging Technologies**: Blockchain can be integrated with other emerging technologies such as IoT and AI to create more sophisticated and efficient payment systems. For example, smart contracts can be used in conjunction with IoT devices to automate payments based on sensor data.

Real-World Examples

1. **Ripple:**
   - **Function**: Ripple provides a blockchain-based payment protocol and digital currency (XRP) designed to facilitate fast and low-cost international money transfers. Ripple's technology reduces settlement times from days to seconds and significantly lowers transaction fees.

2. **Stellar**:
    - **Function**: Stellar is a blockchain platform focused on facilitating cross-border payments and financial inclusion. It enables fast and affordable international transfers by connecting banks, payment systems, and people.
3. **IBM Blockchain World Wire**:
    - **Function**: IBM's World Wire leverages blockchain to streamline cross-border payments by using stablecoins as a bridge currency. This technology facilitates real-time transactions and reduces costs associated with international payments.
4. **BitPesa (now known as AZA Finance)**:
    - **Function**: AZA Finance uses blockchain technology to facilitate faster and more cost-effective cross-border payments and currency exchange, particularly in Africa. It offers solutions for business payments and remittances.
5. **VeChain**:
    - **Function**: VeChain integrates blockchain with supply chain management, providing transparency and efficiency in tracking payments and goods. It automates payment processing through smart contracts and enhances traceability in the supply chain.

Blockchain technology enhances payment processing by offering faster, more secure, and cost-effective solutions. Its ability to automate transactions, reduce intermediary fees, and provide transparency and traceability makes it a powerful tool for modernizing financial services.

5.2 Cross-Border Transfers: *Benefits of blockchain for international money transfers*

Blockchain technology offers transformative benefits for cross-border money transfers, addressing key inefficiencies and challenges typically faced in international transactions. Here's how blockchain enhances the cross-border transfer process:

1. Faster Transactions

- **Near-Instantaneous Settlement**: Traditional cross-border transfers can take several days to process due to the involvement of multiple intermediaries, different time zones, and banking hours. Blockchain allows for near-instantaneous settlement of transactions by recording them on a decentralized ledger, reducing transfer times to minutes or even seconds.
- **24/7 Operation**: Blockchain networks operate continuously, allowing for real-time transactions regardless of business hours or weekends. This eliminates delays associated with traditional banking systems that operate within limited hours.

2. Cost Reduction

- **Elimination of Intermediaries**: Cross-border transfers typically involve multiple intermediaries, such as correspondent banks and payment processors, each of which charges fees. Blockchain reduces or eliminates the need for intermediaries by enabling direct peer-to-peer transactions, significantly lowering transaction fees.
- **Lower Transaction Costs**: By bypassing traditional financial infrastructure and leveraging decentralized networks, blockchain reduces the overall cost of international money transfers. This is particularly beneficial for remittances and small-value transfers.

3. Enhanced Transparency

- **Immutable Ledger**: Blockchain provides a transparent and immutable ledger where every transaction is recorded and cannot be altered or deleted. This transparency ensures that all parties have access to the same information, which helps in tracking and verifying transactions.

- **Audit Trail**: The permanent nature of blockchain records creates a clear audit trail of all transactions. This simplifies compliance with regulatory requirements and enhances accountability by providing an accurate and unchangeable record of transaction details.

4. Increased Security

- **Cryptographic Protection**: Transactions on a blockchain are secured through cryptographic techniques, including hashing and digital signatures. This ensures that transaction data is protected from tampering and unauthorized access.
- **Decentralized Consensus**: Blockchain networks validate transactions through decentralized consensus mechanisms (e.g., Proof of Work, Proof of Stake). This decentralized approach reduces the risk of fraud and manipulation compared to centralized systems.

5. Reduced Risk of Errors

- **Automated Processes**: Smart contracts can automate transaction processes and enforce terms and conditions without human intervention. This reduces the risk of manual errors, discrepancies, and disputes in cross-border transfers.
- **Consistency**: Automated execution ensures consistent application of transaction rules and conditions, minimizing the risk of mistakes that can occur in traditional manual processes.

6. Currency Conversion and Cross-Border Settlement

- **Real-Time Currency Conversion**: Blockchain can facilitate real-time currency conversion using digital currencies or stablecoins. This eliminates delays and complexities associated with currency exchange and settlement in traditional cross-border transactions.

- **Stablecoins**: Stablecoins, which are digital currencies pegged to a stable asset (such as a fiat currency), can be used on blockchain platforms to mitigate currency volatility and provide a stable medium for cross-border transactions.

7. Financial Inclusion

- **Access to Banking Services**: Blockchain technology can provide financial services to underbanked or unbanked populations, particularly in regions with limited access to traditional banking infrastructure. This enables individuals in remote areas to participate in global financial systems.
- **Low-Cost Remittances**: Blockchain offers an efficient and affordable solution for international remittances, which is particularly beneficial for migrant workers sending money back to their families in developing countries.

Real-World Examples

1. **Ripple**:
    - **Function**: Ripple's XRP Ledger is designed for fast and cost-effective cross-border payments. Ripple's network enables instant settlement and currency conversion, reducing the time and cost associated with traditional international transfers.
2. **Stellar**:
    - **Function**: Stellar facilitates cross-border payments and financial inclusion by connecting banks, payment systems, and individuals. Its network supports low-cost transactions and real-time currency

conversion, making it ideal for international money transfers.

3. **IBM World Wire**:
   - **Function**: IBM's World Wire leverages blockchain to streamline cross-border payments. It uses stablecoins as bridge currencies to enable fast, secure, and cost-effective international transactions.

4. **BitPesa (now AZA Finance)**:
   - **Function**: AZA Finance uses blockchain technology to provide efficient cross-border payment solutions, particularly in Africa. It enables businesses to conduct international transactions and currency exchange with reduced fees and faster processing times.

5. **Remitly**:
   - **Function**: Remitly, a digital remittance service, utilizes blockchain to enhance its cross-border transfer services. By integrating blockchain technology, Remitly improves transaction speed, reduces costs, and enhances security for international money transfers.

6. **Singly**:
   - **Function**: Singly offers blockchain-based cross-border payment solutions, focusing on reducing transaction fees and providing real-time settlements. Its platform facilitates efficient international transfers and currency exchange.

7. **Ripple**:
   - **Function**: Ripple's XRP Ledger is designed for fast and cost-effective cross-border payments. Ripple's network enables instant settlement and currency conversion, reducing

the time and cost associated with traditional international transfers.

8. **Stellar**:
    - **Function**: Stellar facilitates cross-border payments and financial inclusion by connecting banks, payment systems, and individuals. Its network supports low-cost transactions and real-time currency conversion, making it ideal for international money transfers.

9. **IBM World Wire**:
    - **Function**: IBM's World Wire leverages blockchain to streamline cross-border payments. It uses stablecoins as bridge currencies to enable fast, secure, and cost-effective international transactions.

10. **BitPesa (now AZA Finance)**:
    - **Function**: AZA Finance uses blockchain technology to provide efficient cross-border payment solutions, particularly in Africa. It enables businesses to conduct international transactions and currency exchange with reduced fees and faster processing times.

11. **Remitly**:
    - **Function**: Remitly, a digital remittance service, utilizes blockchain to enhance its cross-border transfer services. By integrating blockchain technology, Remitly improves transaction speed, reduces costs, and enhances security for international money transfers.

12. **Singly**:
    - **Function**: Singly offers blockchain-based cross-border payment solutions, focusing on reducing transaction fees and providing real-time settlements. Its platform facilitates

> efficient international transfers and currency exchange.
>
> o

Blockchain technology significantly enhances the efficiency of cross-border transfers by providing faster, more secure, and cost-effective solutions. Its ability to automate processes, reduce intermediary costs, and offer transparent and real-time transaction capabilities makes it a valuable tool for modernizing international payment systems.

5.3 Digital Currencies: *Overview of digital currencies and their role in blockchain-based payments*

Digital currencies represent a form of money that exists only in digital form and is used for transactions on electronic systems. They include various types of cryptocurrencies and digital tokens, each with unique characteristics and use cases. In the context of blockchain-based payments, digital currencies play a crucial role in facilitating secure, efficient, and decentralized transactions.

1. Types of Digital Currencies

1. **Cryptocurrencies**
    - **Definition**: Cryptocurrencies are digital or virtual currencies that use cryptographic techniques to secure transactions and control the creation of new units. They operate on decentralized blockchain networks.
    - **Examples**:
        - **Bitcoin (BTC)**: The first and most well-known cryptocurrency, designed as a decentralized digital currency without a central authority.
        - **Ethereum (ETH)**: A cryptocurrency that supports smart contracts and decentralized applications (dApps) on its blockchain.

2. **Stablecoins**
    - **Definition**: Stablecoins are digital currencies pegged to a stable asset, such as a fiat currency (e.g., USD) or a commodity (e.g., gold). They aim to provide price stability and reduce volatility.
    - **Examples**:
        - **Tether (USDT)**: Pegged to the US Dollar, Tether is widely used for trading

and transactions to avoid cryptocurrency volatility.
- **USD Coin (USDC)**: A stablecoin backed by US Dollar reserves, ensuring its value remains stable relative to the Dollar.

3. **Central Bank Digital Currencies (CBDCs)**
   - **Definition**: CBDCs are digital currencies issued and regulated by central banks. They represent a digital form of a country's fiat currency.
   - **Examples**:
     - **Digital Yuan (e-CNY)**: Issued by the People's Bank of China, it aims to modernize the payment system and increase monetary control.
     - **Digital Euro**: The European Central Bank is exploring a digital version of the Euro to enhance payment efficiency and financial inclusion.

4. **Utility Tokens**
   - **Definition**: Utility tokens are digital tokens used within specific blockchain platforms to access or pay for services. They are often issued during Initial Coin Offerings (ICOs) or token sales.
   - **Examples**:
     - **Binance Coin (BNB)**: Used to pay for transaction fees and participate in various services on the Binance Exchange.
     - **Basic Attention Token (BAT)**: Used within the Brave browser ecosystem to reward users for attention and ad engagement.

2. Role of Digital Currencies in Blockchain-Based Payments

1. **Decentralization**

- **Eliminates Intermediaries**: Digital currencies enable direct peer-to-peer transactions without intermediaries such as banks or payment processors. This reduces transaction costs and speeds up payment processes.

2. **Efficiency and Speed**
   - **Faster Transactions**: Digital currencies facilitate faster transactions compared to traditional banking systems, which can be slow and involve several intermediaries. Blockchain transactions can be processed within minutes or even seconds.

3. **Cost Reduction**
   - **Lower Fees**: Transactions using digital currencies generally incur lower fees than traditional financial systems. This is particularly beneficial for international transfers, where traditional fees can be high.

4. **Security**
   - **Cryptographic Security**: Digital currencies use cryptographic techniques to secure transactions and control the creation of new units. This enhances the security of transactions and reduces the risk of fraud.

5. **Transparency**
   - **Immutable Records**: Blockchain technology provides an immutable ledger of all transactions, enhancing transparency and accountability. This helps in verifying transactions and ensuring they are tamper-proof.

6. **Financial Inclusion**
   - **Access to Banking Services**: Digital currencies offer financial services to individuals who lack access to traditional banking infrastructure. This

is especially important in underserved or remote areas.

7. **Programmable Money**
   - **Smart Contracts**: Digital currencies like Ethereum support smart contracts, which are self-executing contracts with the terms of the agreement directly written into code. Smart contracts automate and enforce transaction terms without the need for intermediaries.

8. **Real-World Examples**

   1. **Bitcoin (BTC)**
      - **Function**: Bitcoin is used for various types of transactions, including online purchases and cross-border transfers. It is often referred to as "digital gold" due to its store of value properties.

   2. **Ripple (XRP)**
      - **Function**: Ripple uses its digital currency XRP to facilitate fast and low-cost international money transfers. Ripple's technology is used by financial institutions to enhance cross-border payments.

   3. **Tether (USDT)**
      - **Function**: Tether is widely used in cryptocurrency trading as a stable store of value and to mitigate volatility. It is commonly used in decentralized finance (DeFi) applications for trading and liquidity provision.

   4. **USD Coin (USDC)**
      - **Function**: USDC is used in various financial applications for stable transactions and as a

> hedge against volatility. It is also used for lending and borrowing in DeFi protocols.
>
> 5. **Digital Yuan (e-CNY)**
>   - **Function**: The Digital Yuan is being implemented to streamline domestic transactions and modernize the financial system in China. It aims to provide a secure and efficient alternative to cash and traditional banking services.
>
> 6. **Basic Attention Token (BAT)**
>   - **Function**: BAT is used within the Brave browser ecosystem to reward users for their attention and interactions with ads. It facilitates direct transactions between advertisers and users without intermediaries.

Digital currencies play a transformative role in blockchain-based payments by enhancing efficiency, security, and transparency. They offer significant benefits over traditional payment systems and contribute to the broader adoption of blockchain technology in financial transactions.

6. Blockchain in Asset Management

Blockchain technology is making significant strides in the asset management sector, offering transformative solutions that enhance efficiency, transparency, and security.

Here's how blockchain is being applied in asset management within banking and finance:

1. Tokenization of Assets

Tokenization involves converting physical or digital assets into blockchain-based tokens. These tokens represent ownership or claims on the underlying asset and can be traded or managed on the blockchain. Tokenization offers several benefits:

- **Fractional Ownership:** Assets can be divided into smaller, tradable units, allowing for fractional ownership and broader access to high-value assets.

- **Increased Liquidity:** Tokenized assets can be traded more easily on blockchain platforms, increasing liquidity for traditionally illiquid assets like real estate or fine art.
- **Example: Real Estate Tokenization** – Platforms like **Real Estate Investment Trusts (REITs)** and **Property Coin** use blockchain to tokenize real estate properties, enabling investors to buy and sell fractional shares of real estate assets.

2. Streamlined Settlements and Clearings

Blockchain technology enhances the efficiency of settlement and clearing processes in asset management by providing a decentralized ledger for recording transactions. This reduces the time and cost associated with traditional clearinghouses and intermediaries.

- **Real-Time Settlement:** Transactions are settled in real-time, reducing the typical delay of several days and minimizing counterparty risk.
- **Reduced Costs:** By eliminating intermediaries, blockchain lowers transaction costs associated with clearing and settlement.
- **Example: Northern Trust and Broadridge** – These institutions have explored blockchain solutions for the settlement and clearing of mutual funds and other securities, aiming to reduce operational costs and improve processing times.

3. Enhanced Transparency and Auditability

Blockchain's immutable ledger provides a transparent and verifiable record of all asset transactions. This transparency ensures that all participants have access to the same information, enhancing trust and accountability.

- **Audit Trails:** Every transaction is recorded and time-stamped, creating a clear and permanent audit trail.
- **Regulatory Compliance:** Transparent records facilitate regulatory compliance by providing easy access to transaction data for audits and reporting.

- **Example: The DTCC (Depository Trust & Clearing Corporation)** – DTCC has implemented blockchain solutions to provide a transparent and auditable record of securities transactions, improving oversight and compliance in the financial markets.

4. Improved Portfolio Management

Blockchain technology can enhance portfolio management by providing real-time data and reducing the complexity of managing diverse assets. Smart contracts and blockchain platforms facilitate automated rebalancing and management of investment portfolios.

- **Automated Rebalancing:** Smart contracts can automatically execute trades and rebalance portfolios based on predefined criteria.
- **Real-Time Insights:** Blockchain provides real-time updates on asset performance and market conditions, allowing for more informed investment decisions.
- **Example: BlackRock and Fidelity** – These asset management giants are exploring blockchain technology to improve portfolio management and investment strategies, leveraging real-time data and automated processes.

5. Efficient Fund Distribution

Blockchain simplifies the distribution of investment funds by automating processes and reducing administrative overhead. This is particularly useful for managing mutual funds and other collective investment schemes.

- **Automated Fund Distribution:** Smart contracts can automate the distribution of fund shares and dividends, reducing the need for manual processing.
- **Access to Global Markets:** Blockchain facilitates the seamless distribution of funds across borders, enabling greater access to global investment opportunities.
- **Example: Fund Admin Blockchain Solutions** – Several blockchain platforms are developing solutions for

automating the distribution of investment funds, improving efficiency and reducing costs.

6. Secure and Transparent Voting

Blockchain can be used to conduct secure and transparent shareholder voting and corporate governance. The technology ensures that votes are recorded accurately and cannot be tampered with, enhancing the integrity of the voting process.

- **Tamper-Proof Voting:** Blockchain provides a secure and immutable record of votes, preventing tampering or fraud.
- **Increased Participation:** The technology can simplify the voting process and increase shareholder participation by enabling remote and secure voting.
- **Example: NASDAQ Linq** – NASDAQ's Linq platform uses blockchain technology to facilitate shareholder voting and corporate governance, providing a transparent and secure voting process.

In summary, blockchain technology is revolutionizing asset management in banking and finance by enabling asset tokenization, streamlining settlements and clearings, enhancing transparency, improving portfolio management, facilitating efficient fund distribution, and securing shareholder voting. These advancements lead to increased efficiency, reduced costs, and greater trust in asset management processes.

6.1 Tokenization of Assets: *How blockchain technology is used to tokenize physical and digital assets*

Tokenization refers to the process of converting ownership of real-world or digital assets into digital tokens that can be traded, transferred, or stored on a blockchain. This innovative approach leverages blockchain technology to enhance liquidity, transparency, and efficiency in asset management.

1. Concept of Tokenization
 1. **Definition**
    - **Tokenization** is the creation of a digital representation of an asset, known as a token, on a blockchain. These tokens represent ownership or a stake in the asset and are typically designed to be transferable and divisible.
 2. **Types of Assets**
    - **Physical Assets**: Tangible items such as real estate, art, precious metals, and commodities.
    - **Digital Assets**: Intangible items such as intellectual property, digital currencies, and financial instruments.

2. How Tokenization Works
 1. **Asset Identification**
    - **Physical Assets**: The asset is identified and assessed. Documentation proving ownership and legal title is prepared.
    - **Digital Assets**: The digital asset is identified and its attributes or rights are defined.
 2. **Token Creation**
    - **Issuance**: A digital token is created on a blockchain platform, representing the asset. Each token is linked to the asset's value and attributes.

- **Smart Contracts**: Smart contracts are used to automate the issuance, transfer, and management of tokens. They ensure compliance with legal and operational rules.

3. **Asset Registration**
    - **Physical Assets**: The asset's details are recorded on the blockchain, and the token is issued to represent ownership. The blockchain ledger serves as a public record.
    - **Digital Assets**: The digital asset is registered on the blockchain, and tokens are issued to represent fractional ownership or access rights.

4. **Trading and Transfer**
    - **Transactions**: Tokens representing the asset can be traded or transferred on blockchain platforms. Transactions are recorded on the blockchain, providing transparency and security.

5. **Verification and Compliance**
    - **Audits**: Regular audits ensure that the tokens accurately represent the underlying assets and that legal and regulatory compliance is maintained.

3. Benefits of Tokenization

1. **Increased Liquidity**
    - **Fractional Ownership**: Tokenization allows for the fractional ownership of assets, making it easier to trade and transfer smaller portions of high-value assets.

2. **Enhanced Transparency**
    - **Immutable Records**: Blockchain provides an immutable ledger of all transactions, enhancing transparency and reducing the risk of fraud.

3. **Improved Accessibility**
    - **Global Reach**: Tokenized assets can be accessed and traded on global blockchain platforms,

expanding market reach and investment opportunities.

4. **Efficient Transactions**
   - **Reduced Costs**: Blockchain technology reduces the need for intermediaries, leading to lower transaction costs and faster processing times.

5. **Enhanced Security**
   - **Cryptographic Protection**: Tokens are secured using cryptographic techniques, making them resistant to tampering and unauthorized access.

6. **Automation**
   - **Smart Contracts**: Automate various aspects of asset management, including compliance, dividend distribution, and voting rights.

4. **Real-World Examples**

   1. **Real Estate**
      - **Example**: **Real Estate Investment Platforms** such as **Property** and **Real Estate Investment Trusts (REITs)** use blockchain to tokenize real estate assets, allowing investors to buy and sell fractional ownership of properties. For instance, **Real Estate Token (RET)** offers a platform where properties can be tokenized, allowing investors to trade fractional ownership shares.

   2. **Art and Collectibles**
      - **Example**: **Myco** and **CurioInvest** are platforms that tokenize art pieces and collectibles, allowing investors to own shares in high-value items. **CurioInvest** facilitates the tokenization of collectible items, providing a marketplace for trading fractional ownership.

   3. **Precious Metals**
      - **Example**: **Paxos** and **GoldMint** use blockchain to tokenize precious metals such as

gold. **Paxos** offers **Paxos Standard (PAX)**, a digital token backed by physical gold, which can be traded and redeemed at a fixed rate.

4. **Digital Assets**
   - **Example**: **Non-Fungible Tokens (NFTs)** are used to tokenize digital assets such as digital art, music, and virtual real estate. Platforms like **OpenSea** and **Rarible** enable the creation, trading, and ownership of NFTs representing unique digital items.

5. **Financial Instruments**
   - **Example**: **Securitize** and **Polymath** offer platforms for tokenizing financial securities such as stocks and bonds. **Securitize** allows the issuance of tokenized securities that comply with regulatory standards, providing a platform for trading and managing these assets.

6. **Commodities**
   - **Example**: **DigiGold** and **Goldex** provide platforms for tokenizing commodities like gold, enabling users to trade and invest in commodity-backed tokens. **DigiGold** offers digital tokens backed by physical gold, facilitating easier trading and liquidity.

5. Conclusion

Tokenization is revolutionizing asset management by leveraging blockchain technology to enhance liquidity, transparency, and efficiency. By converting physical and digital assets into digital tokens, stakeholders can benefit from fractional ownership, reduced transaction costs, and improved accessibility. The real-world examples illustrate the practical applications of tokenization across various asset classes, highlighting its transformative potential in the financial and investment sectors.

6.2 Managing Investments with Blockchain: *The impact of blockchain on investment management and securities*

Blockchain technology is transforming investment management and securities through its ability to offer greater transparency, efficiency, and security. By leveraging blockchain, investment management can be more streamlined and effective, addressing long-standing challenges in the sector.

1. Transparency and Security

1. **Immutable Records**
   - **Blockchain Advantage**: Transactions and ownership records on the blockchain are immutable, meaning they cannot be altered once added to the ledger. This ensures a permanent and tamper-proof record of all investment transactions.
   - **Benefit**: Increased transparency and reduced risk of fraud or manipulation, leading to greater trust among investors and stakeholders.
2. **Real-Time Reporting**
   - **Blockchain Advantage**: Blockchain provides real-time updates on transactions and holdings, allowing for instantaneous reporting and verification.
   - **Benefit**: Investors and managers have access to up-to-date information, improving decision-making and operational efficiency.

2. Efficiency and Cost Reduction

1. **Streamlined Transactions**
   - **Blockchain Advantage**: Blockchain eliminates the need for intermediaries such as brokers and clearinghouses by allowing direct peer-to-peer

transactions. Smart contracts can automate and enforce the terms of transactions.
    - **Benefit**: Reduced transaction times and lower costs associated with traditional intermediaries.
2. **Automated Compliance**
    - **Blockchain Advantage**: Smart contracts can automatically enforce compliance with regulatory requirements, such as KYC (Know Your Customer) and AML (Anti-Money Laundering) rules.
    - **Benefit**: Reduced administrative burden and costs related to compliance management.
3. **Enhanced Settlements**
    - **Blockchain Advantage**: Blockchain enables faster settlement times for trades, often reducing the settlement period from days to seconds.
    - **Benefit**: Improved liquidity and reduced risk associated with delayed settlements.

3. Tokenization of Assets

1. **Fractional Ownership**
    - **Blockchain Advantage**: Tokenization allows for the fractional ownership of assets, meaning investors can buy and sell smaller portions of high-value investments.
    - **Benefit**: Increased accessibility and liquidity for assets that were previously difficult to trade in smaller units.
2. **Diversification**
    - **Blockchain Advantage**: Tokenization facilitates access to a broader range of asset classes and investment opportunities, including real estate, art, and commodities.

- **Benefit**: Enhanced portfolio diversification and opportunities for investors to access previously inaccessible markets.

4. Enhanced Liquidity

1. **Secondary Markets**
   - **Blockchain Advantage**: Tokenized assets can be traded on blockchain-based secondary markets, increasing their liquidity compared to traditional asset classes.
   - **Benefit**: Easier entry and exit from investments, improving the overall liquidity of investment portfolios.

2. **Global Reach**
   - **Blockchain Advantage**: Blockchain platforms operate globally, allowing investors from different regions to participate in markets and investments that were previously restricted by geographical barriers.
   - **Benefit**: Access to a global pool of investors and investment opportunities.

5. Improved Investor Experience

1. **Customized Investment Products**
   - **Blockchain Advantage**: Blockchain technology enables the creation of bespoke investment products through smart contracts, tailored to specific investor needs and preferences.
   - **Benefit**: More personalized investment options and better alignment with individual investment goals.

2. **Enhanced Transparency of Fees**
   - **Blockchain Advantage**: Transparent ledgers and smart contracts can clearly outline and enforce fee structures, ensuring investors are fully aware of any costs associated with their investments.

- o **Benefit**: Greater clarity and trust regarding fees and charges.

6. Risk Management
   1. **Fraud Prevention**
      - o **Blockchain Advantage**: The immutability and transparency of blockchain reduce the risk of fraud by providing a clear and verifiable history of all transactions.
      - o **Benefit**: Increased security and reduced risk of fraudulent activities affecting investments.
   2. **Counterparty Risk**
      - o **Blockchain Advantage**: Smart contracts automate and enforce the terms of transactions, reducing reliance on trust between parties and minimizing counterparty risk.
      - o **Benefit**: Reduced risk of default or dispute in transactions.

7. **Real-World Examples**
   1. **tZERO:**
      - o **Description**: tZERO is a blockchain-based platform that provides a decentralized exchange for trading digital securities. It aims to improve the efficiency and transparency of trading and settlement processes.
      - o **Impact**: Facilitates faster and more secure trading of tokenized securities, enhancing liquidity and reducing costs.
   2. **Securitize:**
      - o **Description**: Securitize offers a platform for issuing and managing digital securities through blockchain technology. It automates compliance and investor management through smart contracts.

- o **Impact**: Simplifies the issuance of securities, improves compliance management, and enhances the investor experience.
3. **Real Estate Token (RET):**
    - o **Description**: **RET** tokenizes real estate assets, allowing fractional ownership and trading of property shares on a blockchain platform.
    - o **Impact**: Increases liquidity and accessibility to real estate investments, making it easier for investors to buy and sell property shares.
4. **GoldMint:**
    - o **Description**: **GoldMint** tokenizes physical gold, allowing investors to trade gold-backed tokens on a blockchain platform. Each token represents a specific amount of physical gold stored in secure vaults.
    - o **Impact**: Provides a liquid and accessible way to invest in gold, reducing the need for physical storage and improving trading efficiency.
5. **Polymath:**
    - o **Description**: **Polymath** provides a platform for creating and managing security tokens on the blockchain. It focuses on compliance and regulatory adherence for tokenized securities.
    - o **Impact**: Streamlines the process of issuing and managing security tokens, ensuring compliance with regulatory standards.
6. **CurioInvest:**
    - o **Description**: **CurioInvest** allows for the tokenization of collectible assets and offers a platform for trading and investing in tokenized collectibles.

> - **Impact**: Provides access to high-value collectibles through fractional ownership, enhancing liquidity and market access.

8. Conclusion

Blockchain technology offers significant improvements in investment management and securities by enhancing transparency, reducing costs, and increasing efficiency. Through tokenization, automation, and improved security, blockchain is reshaping how investments are managed, traded, and secured. Real-world examples demonstrate the practical benefits and transformative potential of blockchain in the financial industry. As the technology continues to evolve, its impact on investment management is likely to grow, offering new opportunities for investors and financial institutions alike.

6.3 Real-Time Portfolio Tracking: *Using blockchain for real-time tracking and transparency in asset management*

Blockchain technology offers a revolutionary approach to portfolio tracking and asset management by providing real-time updates and unparalleled transparency. This innovation helps address traditional challenges such as delays in reporting, lack of transparency, and inefficiencies in data handling. Here's how blockchain can transform real-time portfolio tracking and asset management:

1. Instantaneous Updates

1. **Real-Time Data Synchronization**
   - **Blockchain Advantage**: Blockchain enables real-time synchronization of data across all nodes in the network. Each transaction is instantly recorded and updated across the blockchain ledger, providing a live view of portfolio performance.
   - **Benefit**: Investors and asset managers have immediate access to up-to-date information about their portfolios, facilitating prompt decision-making.

2. **Continuous Monitoring**
   - **Blockchain Advantage**: The decentralized nature of blockchain allows continuous monitoring of transactions and portfolio changes, ensuring that any updates or adjustments are reflected in real-time.
   - **Benefit**: Enhances the ability to track portfolio performance and market movements as they happen, leading to more agile investment strategies.

2. Enhanced Transparency
1. **Immutable Records**
   - **Blockchain Advantage**: Blockchain's immutable ledger ensures that all transactions and asset movements are permanently recorded and cannot be altered or erased.
   - **Benefit**: Provides a transparent and verifiable history of all portfolio transactions, reducing the risk of fraud and errors.
2. **Audit Trails**
   - **Blockchain Advantage**: Every transaction on the blockchain is timestamped and linked to previous records, creating a comprehensive audit trail.
   - **Benefit**: Simplifies compliance and auditing processes by providing an easily accessible and detailed record of all activities.

3. Improved Security
1. **Data Integrity**
   - **Blockchain Advantage**: Blockchain uses cryptographic techniques to secure data, ensuring that transactions are encrypted and tamper-proof.
   - **Benefit**: Protects portfolio data from unauthorized access or tampering, enhancing the overall security of asset management systems.
2. **Decentralization**
   - **Blockchain Advantage**: The decentralized nature of blockchain means that data is distributed across multiple nodes, eliminating single points of failure.
   - **Benefit**: Increases resilience against cyberattacks and system failures, ensuring continuous availability of portfolio data.

4. Efficient Transaction Processing

1. **Automated Settlements**
   - **Blockchain Advantage**: Smart contracts on blockchain platforms can automate and enforce the terms of transactions, including settlements and transfers.
   - **Benefit**: Speeds up transaction processing and reduces the need for manual intervention, leading to faster and more efficient portfolio management.

2. **Reduced Costs**
   - **Blockchain Advantage**: By eliminating intermediaries and streamlining processes, blockchain reduces transaction costs and operational expenses.
   - **Benefit**: Lower costs associated with managing and tracking portfolios, improving overall profitability.

5. Portfolio Diversification and Integration

1. **Unified Platform**
   - **Blockchain Advantage**: Blockchain platforms can integrate various asset classes and investment products into a single, unified system.
   - **Benefit**: Allows for seamless tracking and management of diverse portfolios, including traditional and digital assets.

2. **Access to New Markets**
   - **Blockchain Advantage**: Blockchain enables access to new and emerging markets through tokenized assets and global trading platforms.
   - **Benefit**: Facilitates portfolio diversification by providing opportunities to invest in previously inaccessible markets.

7. **Real-World Examples**

   1. **Securitize:**
      - **Description**: **Securitize** offers a platform for managing digital securities on the blockchain, providing real-time tracking and transparency of portfolio holdings.
      - **Impact**: Enables investors to monitor their securities in real time, improving transparency and efficiency in asset management.

   2. **Polymath:**
      - **Description**: **Polymath** facilitates the creation and management of security tokens on the blockchain, offering real-time updates and transparent records of tokenized assets.
      - **Impact**: Enhances the ability to track and manage portfolios of security tokens, improving overall portfolio oversight.

   3. **tZERO:**
      - **Description**: **tZERO** provides a blockchain-based trading platform for digital securities, enabling real-time portfolio tracking and management.
      - **Impact**: Offers investors up-to-date information on their digital securities, enhancing transparency and operational efficiency.

   4. **Harbor:**
      - **Description**: **Harbor** tokenizes private securities and real estate assets, using blockchain for real-time tracking and compliance management.

- **Impact**: Facilitates real-time visibility into the performance and compliance of tokenized assets, improving portfolio management.

5. **CurioInvest:**
    - **Description**: **CurioInvest** tokenizes high-value collectible assets and provides a blockchain-based platform for tracking and trading these assets.
    - **Impact**: Offers real-time tracking and management of collectible assets, enhancing transparency and liquidity.

7. Conclusion

Blockchain technology offers significant advancements in real-time portfolio tracking and asset management by enhancing transparency, security, and efficiency. Through immutable records, automated processes, and real-time data synchronization, blockchain transforms how investors and asset managers monitor and manage their portfolios. Real-world examples demonstrate the practical benefits of blockchain in improving the tracking, transparency, and efficiency of investment management, paving the way for more agile and effective asset management practices.

7. Regulatory and Compliance Considerations

The integration of blockchain technology into banking and finance brings numerous benefits, including enhanced transparency, reduced costs, and increased efficiency.

However, it also introduces a range of regulatory and compliance challenges that must be addressed to ensure the technology's effective and lawful use. Here are key regulatory and compliance considerations for blockchain in banking and finance:

1. Regulatory Frameworks and Legal Recognition

Challenge: Blockchain operates in a decentralized manner, which can complicate the application of existing regulatory frameworks. Different countries have varying regulations regarding cryptocurrencies, smart contracts, and blockchain-based transactions, creating a patchwork of legal standards.

- **Legal Status:** Clarifying the legal status of blockchain-based assets and transactions is crucial. For example, the classification of cryptocurrencies as securities, commodities, or currencies can impact their regulation.
- **International Coordination:** Due to the global nature of blockchain, regulatory bodies need to coordinate internationally to address cross-border challenges and ensure consistent regulatory approaches.
- **Example:** The European Union's **Markets in Crypto-Assets (MiCA)** regulation aims to create a comprehensive regulatory framework for crypto-assets, including stablecoins and utility tokens, to enhance legal clarity and market integrity.

2. Anti-Money Laundering (AML) and Know Your Customer (KYC) Compliance

Challenge: Blockchain's pseudonymous nature can pose challenges for AML and KYC compliance, as it may be difficult to trace and verify the identities of users involved in transactions.

- **KYC Requirements:** Financial institutions using blockchain must implement robust KYC procedures to verify the identities of their clients and prevent illicit activities.
- **AML Controls:** Blockchain platforms need to establish AML controls to monitor and report suspicious activities, ensuring that transactions do not facilitate money laundering or terrorist financing.
- **Example: Chainalysis** and **Elliptic** provide blockchain analytics tools that help institutions comply with AML regulations by offering transaction monitoring and identity verification services.

3. Data Privacy and Protection

Challenge: Blockchain's immutable ledger and transparency features can conflict with data privacy regulations, such as the

General Data Protection Regulation (GDPR) in the European Union, which grants individuals the right to request the deletion of their personal data.

- **Data Erasure:** Implementing mechanisms for data erasure while maintaining the integrity of the blockchain is challenging, as data on the blockchain is designed to be permanent and unalterable.
- **Privacy Compliance:** Organizations must balance blockchain's transparency with privacy requirements, potentially using techniques like zero-knowledge proofs or private blockchains to address privacy concerns.
- **Example:** The **GDPR Compliance Framework** developed by various blockchain consortia outlines strategies for ensuring compliance with data protection regulations while utilizing blockchain technology.

4. Smart Contract Governance and Liability

Challenge: Smart contracts are self-executing contracts with code that automatically enforces the terms of an agreement. Issues related to governance, code errors, and liability must be considered.

- **Governance Models:** Defining governance structures for smart contracts is essential to manage disputes, make amendments, and ensure proper oversight.
- **Liability and Code Bugs:** Establishing liability in case of code bugs or unintended consequences is crucial. Clear terms and conditions must be defined to address potential issues arising from smart contract execution.
- **Example: OpenLaw** and **Legalese** offer platforms for creating and managing legal smart contracts, incorporating legal review processes to address governance and liability issues.

5. Security and Cybersecurity

Challenge: Blockchain technology, while secure, is not immune to cybersecurity risks. Ensuring the security of blockchain networks and protecting against attacks are critical concerns.

- **Network Security:** Implementing robust security measures to protect blockchain networks from attacks such as 51% attacks, double-spending, and smart contract vulnerabilities.
- **Data Integrity:** Ensuring that data stored on the blockchain remains accurate and secure from tampering or unauthorized access.
- **Example:** **IBM's Hyperledger Fabric** provides enterprise-grade blockchain solutions with built-in security features, including encryption and access control, to address cybersecurity concerns.

6. Consumer Protection

Challenge: As blockchain technology introduces new financial products and services, ensuring consumer protection becomes essential.

- **Disclosures and Transparency:** Providing clear and transparent information about blockchain-based products and services to consumers to enable informed decision-making.
- **Dispute Resolution:** Establishing mechanisms for resolving disputes related to blockchain transactions and smart contracts, ensuring fair treatment of consumers.
- **Example: The Financial Conduct Authority (FCA)** in the UK has issued guidelines for consumer protection in the crypto-assets market, emphasizing the importance of transparency and risk disclosures.

7. Taxation and Reporting

Challenge: The tax treatment of blockchain-based transactions and assets can be complex, requiring clarity on reporting and compliance obligations.

- **Tax Reporting:** Establishing guidelines for the taxation of cryptocurrency transactions, capital gains, and income derived from blockchain-based investments.

- **Cross-Border Taxation:** Addressing issues related to cross-border transactions and international tax compliance, considering the global nature of blockchain.
- **Example: CoinTracker** and **Koinly** offer cryptocurrency tax reporting solutions that help users comply with tax regulations by tracking transactions and generating tax reports.

In summary, the integration of blockchain technology into banking and finance necessitates careful consideration of regulatory and compliance issues, including legal recognition, AML/KYC compliance, data privacy, smart contract governance, security, consumer protection, and taxation. Addressing these challenges is crucial for the successful and lawful adoption of blockchain technology in the financial sector.

7.1 Regulatory Frameworks for Blockchain: *Key regulations and standards affecting blockchain in banking and finance*

As blockchain technology continues to evolve and become integrated into banking and finance, regulatory frameworks and standards are essential for ensuring its safe and effective use. Different jurisdictions have developed various regulations to address the unique challenges and opportunities presented by blockchain technology. Here's an overview of key regulations and standards affecting blockchain in the banking and finance sector:

1. Global Regulatory Standards

1. **Financial Action Task Force (FATF)**
   - **Overview**: FATF is an international body that sets standards for anti-money laundering (AML) and counter-terrorist financing (CTF) efforts.
   - **Impact on Blockchain**: FATF guidelines include recommendations for virtual asset service providers (VASPs) to adhere to AML and CTF measures, including Know Your Customer (KYC) requirements and transaction monitoring.

2. **International Organization for Standardization (ISO)**
   - **Overview**: ISO develops and publishes international standards for a wide range of industries, including finance and technology.
   - **Impact on Blockchain**: ISO standards, such as ISO/TC 307 for blockchain and distributed ledger technologies, provide guidelines for blockchain interoperability, security, and privacy.

2. Regional and National Regulations

1. **European Union (EU)**
   - **General Data Protection Regulation (GDPR)**

- **Overview**: GDPR regulates the processing of personal data within the EU.
- **Impact on Blockchain**: GDPR's requirements for data protection and privacy apply to blockchain implementations, especially regarding the right to erasure and data immutability.
  - **Markets in Crypto-Assets (MiCA) Regulation**
    - **Overview**: MiCA is a comprehensive regulatory framework proposed to govern crypto-assets and related services across the EU.
    - **Impact on Blockchain**: MiCA aims to provide legal clarity on crypto-assets, including stablecoins and utility tokens, ensuring investor protection and market integrity.

2. **United States**
   - **Securities and Exchange Commission (SEC)**
     - **Overview**: SEC regulates securities markets and enforces securities laws.
     - **Impact on Blockchain**: SEC's guidance addresses how blockchain-based tokens may be classified as securities and thus subject to securities regulations. The SEC also focuses on the protection of investors in Initial Coin Offerings (ICOs).
   - **Commodity Futures Trading Commission (CFTC)**
     - **Overview**: CFTC regulates commodity futures and options markets.

- **Impact on Blockchain**: CFTC has jurisdiction over cryptocurrency derivatives and futures contracts, providing oversight on trading activities involving blockchain-based assets.
        - Financial Crimes Enforcement Network (FinCEN)
            - **Overview**: FinCEN enforces AML and CTF regulations in the U.S.
            - **Impact on Blockchain**: FinCEN's regulations require blockchain-based platforms to implement AML practices, including reporting suspicious activities and maintaining KYC procedures.

3. **China**
    - **Overview**: China has implemented strict regulations on cryptocurrency trading and Initial Coin Offerings (ICOs), while promoting blockchain technology for various applications.
    - **Impact on Blockchain**: The Chinese government restricts cryptocurrency exchanges and ICO activities but supports blockchain research and development, especially for financial applications like digital currency issuance.

4. **Japan**
    - Financial Services Agency (FSA)
        - **Overview**: FSA regulates financial markets and services in Japan.
        - **Impact on Blockchain**: Japan has established a legal framework for cryptocurrency exchanges, requiring registration and adherence to AML regulations. The FSA also regulates

stablecoins and digital asset custody services.

5. **Singapore**
   - **Monetary Authority of Singapore (MAS)**
     - **Overview**: MAS is Singapore's central bank and financial regulatory authority.
     - **Impact on Blockchain**: MAS provides a regulatory framework for digital payment token services and has issued guidelines for ICOs and digital asset trading, focusing on investor protection and market integrity.

3. Industry Standards and Guidelines

1. **Blockchain Security Guidelines**
   - **Overview**: Industry groups and organizations provide guidelines for securing blockchain networks and applications.
   - **Impact on Blockchain**: These guidelines cover best practices for securing blockchain systems, including cryptographic techniques, network security, and vulnerability management.

2. **Data Privacy Standards**
   - **Overview**: Standards related to data privacy, such as ISO/IEC 27001 for information security management.
   - **Impact on Blockchain**: Ensures that blockchain implementations adhere to privacy standards and protect sensitive information in compliance with global data protection regulations.

4. Emerging Trends

1. **Decentralized Finance (DeFi) Regulations**

- **Overview**: As DeFi platforms grow, regulators are developing frameworks to address the risks associated with decentralized financial services.
- **Impact on Blockchain**: Emerging regulations aim to ensure that DeFi platforms adhere to financial regulations, including AML and investor protection requirements.

2. **Stablecoin Regulations**
    - **Overview**: With the rise of stablecoins, regulatory bodies are focusing on establishing rules for their issuance and usage.
    - **Impact on Blockchain**: Regulations are being developed to address the risks associated with stablecoins, including their impact on monetary policy and financial stability.

6. **Real-World Examples**
    1. **Coinbase**
        - **Description**: A major cryptocurrency exchange based in the U.S. that complies with SEC and FinCEN regulations.
        - **Regulatory Impact**: Coinbase adheres to AML/KYC requirements and reports suspicious activities, ensuring regulatory compliance in its operations.
    2. **Binance**
        - **Description**: A global cryptocurrency exchange that operates in multiple jurisdictions.
        - **Regulatory Impact**: Binance has adapted its operations to comply with various national regulations, including those set by the EU and Asian countries.
    3. **Ripple**

- **Description**: A blockchain-based payment protocol that facilitates cross-border transactions.
- **Regulatory Impact**: Ripple's XRP token has faced scrutiny from the SEC, highlighting the need for clarity in regulations concerning digital tokens and their classification.

4. **Ethereum**
   - **Description**: A decentralized blockchain platform that supports smart contracts and dApps.
   - **Regulatory Impact**: Ethereum's use of smart contracts has influenced regulatory discussions on how decentralized applications should be governed.

5. **Facebook's Diem (formerly Libra)**
   - **Description**: A proposed digital currency project by Facebook aimed at creating a global stablecoin.
   - **Regulatory Impact**: Diem has faced significant regulatory scrutiny from global financial authorities, highlighting the challenges of integrating new digital currencies into existing regulatory frameworks.

Regulatory frameworks for blockchain in banking and finance are evolving to address the unique challenges posed by this technology. By establishing clear guidelines for security, transparency, and compliance, regulators aim to ensure that blockchain applications are integrated safely and effectively into the financial system. The examples provided illustrate how various jurisdictions and organizations are navigating the regulatory landscape, emphasizing the importance of adapting to regulatory requirements in the rapidly advancing blockchain space.

Regulatory Frameworks for Blockchain in India

As blockchain technology gains traction in India, regulatory frameworks are crucial to managing its integration into the banking and finance sectors. India has seen significant developments in blockchain regulation, with various authorities addressing the unique aspects of this technology. Here's an overview of key regulations, standards, and developments affecting blockchain in banking and finance in India:

1. Government and Regulatory Bodies

1. **Reserve Bank of India (RBI)**
    - **Overview**: The RBI is India's central bank and primary regulator for banking and financial institutions.
    - **Impact on Blockchain**: The RBI has issued guidelines affecting cryptocurrency transactions and digital assets. In 2018, the RBI imposed a banking ban on cryptocurrency transactions, which was later lifted by the Supreme Court in 2020. The RBI is also exploring the potential of central bank digital currencies (CBDCs).

2. **Securities and Exchange Board of India (SEBI)**
    - **Overview**: SEBI regulates securities markets and protects investor interests.
    - **Impact on Blockchain**: SEBI's regulations impact the use of blockchain for securities trading and Initial Coin Offerings (ICOs). SEBI has provided guidelines for public and private blockchain-based token offerings and their regulatory compliance.

3. **Ministry of Finance**
    - **Overview**: The Ministry of Finance is involved in policy-making for financial regulations in India.

- Impact on Blockchain: The Ministry has been part of discussions regarding the regulatory framework for cryptocurrencies and blockchain technologies, including potential legislation and policy guidelines.

4. **National Payments Corporation of India (NPCI)**
    - **Overview**: NPCI operates the national financial payment systems in India.
    - **Impact on Blockchain**: NPCI has explored blockchain for enhancing payment systems and fraud prevention. It is involved in initiatives to integrate blockchain technology with existing payment infrastructure.

5. **Department of Economic Affairs (DEA)**
    - **Overview**: DEA is part of the Ministry of Finance and is involved in economic policy-making.
    - **Impact on Blockchain**: DEA has been involved in discussions regarding the regulation of cryptocurrencies and the potential introduction of a digital rupee.

2. Regulatory Developments and Frameworks

1. **Cryptocurrency and Regulation of Official Digital Currency Bill, 2021**
    - **Overview**: This bill proposes a regulatory framework for cryptocurrencies and aims to create a central bank digital currency (CBDC).
    - **Impact on Blockchain**: The bill seeks to ban private cryptocurrencies while allowing the RBI to issue a digital rupee. It outlines provisions for regulating crypto transactions and protecting investors.

2. **Digital Rupee (CBDC)**

- **Overview**: The RBI has expressed interest in issuing a digital version of the Indian rupee.
- **Impact on Blockchain**: The digital rupee would use blockchain technology to facilitate secure and efficient transactions, enhancing the overall financial infrastructure.

3. **Regulations for Crypto Exchanges**
    - **Overview**: Various state and national guidelines impact the operation of cryptocurrency exchanges.
    - **Impact on Blockchain**: Regulations require exchanges to adhere to Anti-Money Laundering (AML) and Know Your Customer (KYC) norms. Compliance with these regulations ensures the legality and security of crypto transactions.

4. **IT Act and Data Protection Laws**
    - **Overview**: The Information Technology Act, 2000, and data protection laws impact how blockchain technology is implemented with respect to data privacy and security.
    - **Impact on Blockchain**: These laws require that blockchain applications comply with data protection standards and ensure secure handling of personal data.

3. Industry Standards and Guidelines

1. **National Blockchain Framework**
    - **Overview**: The Indian government has discussed developing a national blockchain framework to standardize blockchain applications across various sectors.
    - **Impact on Blockchain**: A national framework would provide guidelines for blockchain implementation, including best practices for security, privacy, and interoperability.

2. **ISO Standards**
   - **Overview**: International standards, such as ISO/TC 307 for blockchain and distributed ledger technologies, are relevant in the Indian context.
   - **Impact on Blockchain**: These standards provide guidelines for the implementation of blockchain technology in a secure and interoperable manner, influencing Indian blockchain projects and applications.

4. Emerging Trends

1. **Decentralized Finance (DeFi)**
   - **Overview**: DeFi platforms are gaining attention in India for their potential to disrupt traditional financial services.
   - **Impact on Blockchain**: Regulatory bodies are considering how to address the risks and opportunities of DeFi, including regulatory compliance and investor protection.

2. **Blockchain for Supply Chain and Finance**
   - **Overview**: Blockchain is being explored for its applications in supply chain management and financial services.
   - **Impact on Blockchain**: The adoption of blockchain in these areas could lead to increased transparency, efficiency, and security in financial transactions and supply chain operations.

5. **Real-World Examples**

   1. **WazirX**
      - **Description**: A leading cryptocurrency exchange in India.
      - **Regulatory Impact**: WazirX complies with Indian regulations on cryptocurrency exchanges, including AML and KYC

requirements. It also collaborates with the government on blockchain initiatives.

2. **Primechain Technologies**
   - **Description**: A blockchain-based platform focusing on secure document management and verification.
   - **Regulatory Impact**: Primechain's solutions comply with Indian data protection laws and provide secure document handling in line with regulatory requirements.

3. **IIT Kharagpur's Blockchain Research**
   - **Description**: Indian Institute of Technology (IIT) Kharagpur conducts research on blockchain applications.
   - **Regulatory Impact**: IIT Kharagpur's research contributes to the development of blockchain solutions that align with Indian regulatory standards and promote innovative applications.

4. **Government of India's Blockchain Initiatives**
   - **Description**: The Indian government has explored blockchain for various applications, including land records and digital identity.
   - **Regulatory Impact**: These initiatives demonstrate the government's commitment to integrating blockchain technology into public services while adhering to regulatory frameworks.

5. **Ripple's Partnership with Indian Banks**
   - **Description**: Ripple, a blockchain-based payment platform, has collaborated with Indian banks for cross-border payments.
   - **Regulatory Impact**: Ripple's integration with Indian banks adheres to regulatory guidelines

	and enhances the efficiency of international money transfers.

Conclusion

India's regulatory framework for blockchain is evolving to address the complexities of this technology in the banking and finance sectors. By developing comprehensive regulations and standards, India aims to ensure the safe and effective use of blockchain while fostering innovation. The examples provided illustrate how blockchain technology is being integrated into various aspects of India's financial ecosystem, highlighting the importance of regulatory compliance and adaptability in this rapidly advancing field.

7.2 Compliance Challenges: *Common challenges faced by financial institutions in complying with blockchain regulations*

Financial institutions integrating blockchain technology encounter several compliance challenges. These challenges arise due to the complex and evolving nature of blockchain technology, which intersects with various regulatory requirements and standards. Below are some of the primary compliance challenges faced by financial institutions:

1. Regulatory Uncertainty and Fragmentation

- **Challenge**: The regulatory landscape for blockchain and cryptocurrencies is still developing and can vary significantly between jurisdictions. Financial institutions often face uncertainty about which regulations apply and how they will evolve.
- **Impact**: This uncertainty can lead to difficulties in ensuring compliance with current laws and anticipating future regulatory changes. Institutions may struggle to align their operations with inconsistent or rapidly changing regulations.

2. Data Privacy and Security

- **Challenge**: Blockchain technology's transparency and immutability pose unique challenges for data privacy. Regulations such as the General Data Protection Regulation (GDPR) require that personal data be protected and allow for data deletion, which can conflict with blockchain's immutable nature.
- **Impact**: Financial institutions must navigate how to ensure compliance with data privacy laws while leveraging the transparency and security features of blockchain technology. This can involve complex legal and technical adjustments to balance privacy requirements with blockchain's characteristics.

3. Anti-Money Laundering (AML) and Know Your Customer (KYC) Compliance

- **Challenge**: Blockchain's pseudonymous nature can complicate AML and KYC compliance. Financial institutions need to ensure that transactions are transparent and that they can identify and verify users effectively.
- **Impact**: Institutions must implement robust systems to monitor and verify transactions and user identities on blockchain networks. This includes integrating blockchain-based solutions with existing AML and KYC processes and ensuring compliance with both local and international standards.

4. Integration with Legacy Systems

- **Challenge**: Financial institutions often operate with legacy systems that may not be compatible with blockchain technology. Integrating blockchain solutions with these existing systems can be complex and costly.
- **Impact**: Institutions face technical and operational challenges in ensuring that blockchain systems work seamlessly with legacy infrastructure. This may require significant investment in technology upgrades and system integration.

5. Smart Contract Legality and Enforcement

- **Challenge**: Smart contracts, which execute automatically based on predefined rules, raise questions about their legal enforceability and the jurisdiction applicable to their execution.
- **Impact**: Financial institutions must address legal concerns related to the enforceability of smart contracts and ensure that these contracts comply with existing legal frameworks. They may also need to work with legal experts to develop frameworks that recognize and enforce smart contracts.

6. Cross-Border Regulatory Compliance

- **Challenge**: Blockchain technology often operates across borders, which can complicate compliance with different national regulations. Different countries have varying rules regarding blockchain, cryptocurrencies, and data protection.
- **Impact**: Financial institutions need to navigate and comply with a patchwork of international regulations, which can be challenging and resource-intensive. Ensuring compliance across multiple jurisdictions requires careful coordination and legal expertise.

7. Auditability and Transparency

- **Challenge**: Ensuring that blockchain systems are auditable and that transactions can be tracked and verified while maintaining the privacy and security of sensitive data is a key challenge.
- **Impact**: Institutions must implement mechanisms for auditing blockchain transactions and ensuring that regulatory authorities can access necessary information without compromising the integrity of the blockchain.

8. Security and Risk Management

- **Challenge**: Blockchain systems are not immune to security threats. Institutions must manage risks related to smart contract vulnerabilities, 51% attacks, and other blockchain-specific threats.
- **Impact**: Financial institutions need to implement comprehensive security measures and risk management strategies to protect blockchain systems from potential threats and ensure that they comply with relevant security regulations.

9. Regulatory Reporting and Documentation

- **Challenge**: Blockchain's decentralized nature can make regulatory reporting and documentation more complex. Institutions need to ensure that they can generate required reports and maintain proper documentation for compliance purposes.

- **Impact**: Developing systems for regulatory reporting and documentation that align with blockchain technology's unique characteristics requires significant effort and investment.

Real-World Examples

1. **Binance and Regulatory Challenges**
   - **Description**: Binance, a major cryptocurrency exchange, has faced regulatory scrutiny in multiple countries due to issues related to AML and KYC compliance.
   - **Impact**: The exchange has had to adapt its operations to meet regulatory requirements in various jurisdictions, highlighting the challenge of maintaining compliance across different regulatory environments.

2. **Ripple's Legal Disputes**
   - **Description**: Ripple Labs has faced legal challenges from the U.S. Securities and Exchange Commission (SEC) over the classification of its XRP token.
   - **Impact**: The case underscores the difficulties in navigating regulatory uncertainty and the need for clear regulatory frameworks to address the legal status of blockchain assets.

3. **JPMorgan Chase and Blockchain Integration**
   - **Description**: JPMorgan Chase has developed its own blockchain-based payment system, JPM Coin, to streamline transactions and ensure regulatory compliance.
   - **Impact**: The bank's efforts highlight the complexities of integrating blockchain with

4. **Wells Fargo and Data Privacy Issues**
    - **Description**: Wells Fargo has explored blockchain for various applications, including cross-border payments, while addressing data privacy concerns.
    - **Impact**: The bank's experience illustrates the challenge of balancing blockchain's transparency with data privacy requirements and ensuring compliance with regulations like GDPR.

5. **Deutsche Bank and AML Compliance**
    - **Description**: Deutsche Bank has faced scrutiny for its involvement in facilitating transactions for clients with ties to money laundering, emphasizing the need for robust AML compliance in blockchain systems.
    - **Impact**: The bank's challenges underscore the importance of integrating effective AML practices with blockchain technology to meet regulatory requirements.

Conclusion

Financial institutions face several compliance challenges when integrating blockchain technology into their operations. Addressing these challenges requires a comprehensive approach that includes understanding regulatory requirements, implementing robust security measures, and ensuring effective integration with existing systems. By navigating these complexities, institutions can leverage blockchain's benefits while maintaining regulatory compliance.

7.3 Best Practices for Compliance: *Steps to ensure compliance with regulatory requirements in blockchain applications*

Compliance with regulatory requirements is crucial for the successful deployment and operation of blockchain applications, especially in sectors like banking and finance. To ensure adherence to regulations, organizations should adopt the following best practices:

1. Understand Regulatory Requirements

1. **Detailed Regulatory Research:** Start by conducting thorough research to understand the specific regulatory requirements applicable to blockchain applications in your jurisdiction. This includes laws related to anti-money laundering (AML), know your customer (KYC), data protection, securities regulation, and financial transactions.

2. **Consult Legal Experts:** Engage legal experts who specialize in blockchain and financial regulations to ensure you have a comprehensive understanding of applicable rules and guidelines. They can help interpret complex regulations and provide tailored advice.

3. **Example: The European Union's GDPR** and **MiCA (Markets in Crypto-Assets)** regulations provide specific guidelines for data privacy and cryptocurrency activities, respectively. Understanding these regulations is essential for compliance in the EU.

2. Implement Robust KYC and AML Procedures

1. **Enhanced Due Diligence:** Develop and implement comprehensive KYC procedures to verify the identity of users and counterparties. This includes collecting and verifying identification documents and performing background checks.

2. **AML Controls:** Establish AML controls to monitor transactions for suspicious activities. Use blockchain

analytics tools to track and analyze transaction patterns, ensuring that any unusual or potentially illicit activities are flagged and reported.

3. **Example: Chainalysis** and **Elliptic** offer blockchain analytics tools that assist in implementing AML controls by providing transaction monitoring and risk assessment capabilities.

3. Ensure Data Privacy and Protection

1. **Compliance with Data Protection Laws:** Implement measures to ensure compliance with data protection regulations such as GDPR. This includes providing users with control over their personal data, implementing data encryption, and establishing processes for data erasure if necessary.

2. **Privacy by Design:** Incorporate privacy-by-design principles into blockchain applications, ensuring that data protection is considered from the outset of development. Use techniques like zero-knowledge proofs to enhance privacy while maintaining transparency.

3. **Example: The GDPR Compliance Framework** outlines strategies for balancing data privacy with blockchain's transparency features, helping organizations adhere to data protection laws.

4. Develop and Enforce Smart Contract Governance

1. **Clear Governance Framework:** Establish a governance framework for smart contracts that outlines how they will be managed, updated, and enforced. Define roles and responsibilities for monitoring and managing smart contracts.

2. **Code Audits and Testing:** Regularly audit and test smart contract code to identify and address vulnerabilities or bugs. Engage third-party auditors to ensure the code meets security and regulatory standards.

3. **Example: OpenLaw** and **Legalese** provide platforms for creating and managing legal smart contracts,

incorporating governance and auditing processes to ensure compliance and reliability.

5. Implement Security Best Practices

1. **Network Security:** Use robust security measures to protect blockchain networks from attacks, such as 51% attacks and double-spending. Implement multi-signature wallets and cryptographic techniques to enhance security.

2. **Regular Security Assessments:** Conduct regular security assessments and penetration testing to identify and mitigate potential vulnerabilities. Stay updated on emerging threats and adapt security measures accordingly.

3. **Example: IBM Hyperledger Fabric** offers enterprise-grade blockchain solutions with built-in security features, including encryption and access control, to address cybersecurity concerns.

6. Establish Clear Compliance and Reporting Processes

1. **Compliance Documentation:** Maintain comprehensive documentation of compliance procedures, including KYC/AML policies, data protection measures, and smart contract governance. Ensure that these documents are regularly reviewed and updated.

2. **Regular Reporting:** Implement regular reporting mechanisms to provide transparency and accountability. Report any compliance breaches or anomalies to the relevant regulatory authorities in a timely manner.

3. **Example: CoinTracker** and **Koinly** offer cryptocurrency tax reporting solutions that assist users in generating accurate tax reports and complying with reporting requirements.

7. Stay Informed and Adapt

1. **Monitor Regulatory Changes:** Continuously monitor changes in regulations and industry standards. Adapt your compliance practices to align with new or updated regulations, ensuring ongoing adherence.

2. **Engage with Regulatory Bodies:** Participate in industry forums and engage with regulatory bodies to stay informed about regulatory developments and provide feedback on emerging regulations.

3. **Example: The Financial Action Task Force (FATF)** provides guidelines and updates on AML regulations related to cryptocurrencies, helping organizations stay informed about compliance requirements.

8. Educate and Train Staff

1. **Regular Training:** Provide regular training for staff on compliance requirements, regulatory updates, and best practices for using blockchain technology. Ensure that employees understand their roles and responsibilities in maintaining compliance.

2. **Awareness Programs:** Implement awareness programs to keep staff informed about the potential risks associated with blockchain applications and the importance of adhering to regulatory standards.

3. **Example: The Blockchain Training Alliance** offers educational resources and training programs for professionals in the blockchain industry, helping organizations ensure their staff are well-versed in compliance and regulatory matters.

By implementing these best practices, organizations can effectively navigate the regulatory landscape and ensure compliance with relevant laws and guidelines while leveraging the benefits of blockchain technology in banking and finance.

8. Blockchain in Fraud Prevention

Blockchain technology is revolutionizing fraud prevention across various industries by providing an immutable, transparent, and decentralized system for recording transactions.

Here's how blockchain helps in preventing fraud and enhancing security:

1. Immutable Ledger

Tamper-Proof Record: Blockchain's core feature is its immutable ledger, which means once data is recorded on the blockchain, it cannot be altered or deleted without altering all subsequent blocks, which requires consensus from the network. This immutability makes it extremely difficult for fraudsters to manipulate transaction records or falsify information.

Transaction Integrity: Each block in the blockchain contains a cryptographic hash of the previous block, creating a chain of blocks that ensures the integrity of the entire transaction history. This feature is particularly valuable in preventing data tampering and ensuring the accuracy of financial records.

Example: Bitcoin and **Ethereum** use blockchain's immutability to maintain a secure record of all transactions, making it nearly impossible for malicious actors to alter transaction histories.

2. Enhanced Transparency

Public Ledger Access: Many blockchain platforms operate on public ledgers that allow all participants to view and verify transactions in real-time. This transparency ensures that transactions are visible and verifiable by all network participants, reducing the risk of fraudulent activities going unnoticed.

Auditability: The transparent nature of blockchain allows for easy auditing and verification of transactions. Regulators and auditors can access the blockchain ledger to trace and review transactions, enhancing oversight and accountability.

Example: Ripple provides a transparent ledger for cross-border transactions, allowing all parties involved to track and verify transaction details, reducing the risk of fraud in international payments.

3. Decentralized Verification

Consensus Mechanisms: Blockchain uses consensus mechanisms (e.g., Proof of Work, Proof of Stake) to validate and agree on the state of the ledger. This decentralized approach reduces the risk of single points of failure and fraud, as altering transaction data would require controlling a majority of the network nodes.

Distributed Trust: By decentralizing transaction verification across multiple nodes, blockchain eliminates the reliance on a single trusted authority, reducing the risk of collusion or fraud from a centralized entity.

Example: Ethereum employs a decentralized consensus mechanism to validate transactions and smart contracts, ensuring that all participants agree on the validity of transactions and reducing the likelihood of fraudulent activities.

4. Smart Contracts for Automated Enforcement

Self-Executing Agreements: Smart contracts are self-executing contracts with the terms written into code. They automatically enforce and execute the terms of agreements based on predefined conditions, reducing the need for intermediaries and minimizing the risk of human error or manipulation.

Fraud Prevention: Smart contracts can include built-in fraud prevention measures, such as automatic validation of transaction conditions and automatic cancellation of fraudulent or non-compliant transactions.

Example: Chainlink integrates smart contracts with external data sources to provide automated, secure, and transparent execution of contracts, reducing the potential for fraud in various applications, including insurance and supply chain management.

5. Identity Verification and Access Control

Digital Identity Management: Blockchain can be used to create and manage digital identities that are secure, verifiable, and tamper-proof. This enhances the accuracy and reliability of identity verification processes, reducing the risk of identity theft and fraud.

Access Control: Blockchain-based identity solutions can provide secure access control mechanisms, ensuring that only authorized individuals can access sensitive information or perform transactions.

Example: U-Port and **SelfKey** are blockchain-based identity management platforms that allow users to control and verify their digital identities securely, reducing the risk of fraud related to identity theft and unauthorized access.

6. Supply Chain Integrity

Traceability and Provenance: Blockchain enhances supply chain transparency by providing a secure and immutable record of each step in the supply chain. This allows for the tracking of goods from origin to destination, reducing the risk of counterfeit products and fraud.

Verification of Authenticity: Blockchain can verify the authenticity of products and transactions by recording every transaction and movement in the supply chain, ensuring that products are genuine and have not been tampered with.

Example: VeChain uses blockchain technology to track and verify the authenticity of products in supply chains, such as luxury goods and pharmaceuticals, reducing the risk of counterfeit products and fraud.

7. Fraud Detection through Analytics

Transaction Monitoring: Blockchain analytics tools can monitor and analyze transaction patterns to detect suspicious activities and potential fraud. By examining transaction data on the blockchain, these tools can identify anomalies and alert stakeholders to potential fraudulent activities.

Pattern Recognition: Advanced analytics and machine learning algorithms can be applied to blockchain data to recognize patterns indicative of fraudulent behavior, enhancing the ability to detect and prevent fraud.

Example: Elliptic and **Chainalysis** provide blockchain analytics services that help organizations detect and prevent fraud by analyzing transaction patterns and identifying suspicious activities.

In summary, blockchain technology enhances fraud prevention by offering an immutable ledger, improved transparency, decentralized verification, smart contract automation, secure identity management, supply chain integrity, and advanced analytics. These features collectively contribute to a more secure and trustworthy financial ecosystem, reducing the risk of fraud and increasing overall confidence in blockchain-based systems.

Real-World Examples

1. **JPMorgan Chase's Interbank Information Network (IIN)**

- **Description**: JPMorgan Chase's IIN, built on blockchain technology, facilitates secure and transparent cross-border payments by providing real-time transaction visibility.
- **Impact**: The IIN helps prevent fraud by improving the accuracy and speed of transaction processing and reducing the potential for fraudulent activities in international payments.

2. **De Beers and Everledger**
    - **Description**: De Beers, in partnership with Everledger, uses blockchain to track the provenance of diamonds and ensure their authenticity.
    - **Impact**: Blockchain's immutable ledger helps prevent fraud in the diamond industry by verifying the origin and history of diamonds, thus reducing the risk of conflict diamonds entering the market.

3. **Walmart's Blockchain for Supply Chain**
    - **Description**: Walmart uses blockchain technology to enhance transparency and traceability in its supply chain, including tracking the provenance of food products.
    - **Impact**: By using blockchain, Walmart can detect and prevent fraud related to food safety and quality, ensuring that products are accurately represented and reducing the risk of counterfeit goods entering the supply chain.

4. **IBM's Blockchain-Based KYC Solutions**
    - **Description**: IBM has developed blockchain-based solutions for Know Your Customer (KYC) processes to improve identity verification and reduce fraud.

- o **Impact**: These solutions streamline and secure KYC procedures by providing a transparent and immutable record of customer identities, reducing the risk of identity fraud.

5. **HSBC's Blockchain-Based Trade Finance**
   - o **Description**: HSBC has implemented blockchain technology in trade finance to enhance transparency and reduce fraud in trade transactions.
   - o **Impact**: Blockchain improves the accuracy and security of trade finance transactions by providing a decentralized and immutable ledger, reducing the risk of fraudulent trade documents and activities.

8.1 Immutable Records: *The role of blockchain's immutability in preventing fraudulent activities*

Blockchain technology's immutability is one of its most defining and powerful features. Immutability refers to the property of a blockchain that ensures once data has been recorded onto the blockchain, it cannot be altered or deleted. This characteristic plays a crucial role in preventing fraudulent activities across various sectors, especially in banking and finance.

Key Aspects of Blockchain Immutability

1. **Unalterable Transaction History**
   - **Description**: Once a transaction is added to a blockchain, it becomes part of a permanent record. Each block contains a cryptographic hash of the previous block, forming a chain that is nearly impossible to alter without changing all subsequent blocks.
   - **Impact on Fraud Prevention**: This creates a permanent, tamper-proof ledger that provides a clear and unchangeable record of all transactions. Fraudsters cannot retroactively alter transaction details, thus ensuring the integrity of financial records.

2. **Data Integrity and Trust**
   - **Description**: Blockchain's immutability guarantees that data remains consistent and trustworthy. The cryptographic algorithms used in blockchain ensure that once data is recorded, any attempt to alter it will result in a change in the hash value, signaling tampering.
   - **Impact on Fraud Prevention**: Financial institutions and stakeholders can trust the data stored on the blockchain because it is resistant to tampering. This reduces the risk of fraudulent

activities such as forgery or falsification of transaction records.

3. **Audit Trails**
    - **Description**: Every transaction added to the blockchain is time-stamped and linked to previous transactions. This creates an auditable trail of all actions taken on the blockchain.
    - **Impact on Fraud Prevention**: An immutable audit trail allows for comprehensive tracking and verification of transactions. Financial institutions can trace the history of transactions, investigate suspicious activities, and ensure compliance with regulations.

4. **Prevention of Double Spending**
    - **Description**: Blockchain technology uses consensus mechanisms to prevent double spending, where the same digital asset is spent more than once.
    - **Impact on Fraud Prevention**: By ensuring that each transaction is verified and recorded uniquely, blockchain prevents double spending and ensures that digital assets are not fraudulently duplicated or reused.

5. **Transparency and Verification**
    - **Description**: Blockchain's immutability is coupled with transparency. All participants in the blockchain network can access and verify the transaction records.
    - **Impact on Fraud Prevention**: Transparency combined with immutability allows stakeholders to verify transactions independently, reducing the risk of fraudulent activities and enhancing accountability.

6. **Resistance to Unauthorized Changes**

- **Description**: The decentralized nature of blockchain means that altering a single block requires changing all subsequent blocks across all nodes in the network, which is computationally infeasible.
- **Impact on Fraud Prevention**: This resistance to unauthorized changes deters malicious actors from attempting to alter transaction records or manipulate financial data.

Real-World Examples of Blockchain's Immutability in Preventing Fraud

1. **De Beers' Diamond Tracking**
    - **Description**: De Beers uses blockchain to track the provenance of diamonds from mine to market, ensuring they are conflict-free.
    - **Impact**: The immutable ledger prevents tampering with the diamond's history, thereby reducing the risk of conflict diamonds entering the market.

2. **IBM Food Trust**
    - **Description**: IBM's Food Trust blockchain solution tracks the supply chain of food products, from farm to table.
    - **Impact**: The immutable records help prevent fraud related to food safety and quality by ensuring transparency and traceability throughout the supply chain.

3. **Everledger's Asset Tracking**
    - **Description**: Everledger uses blockchain to create a digital ledger for high-value assets, including diamonds, art, and wine.
    - **Impact**: The immutability of blockchain records helps prevent fraud by ensuring that

asset provenance and ownership details cannot be altered.

4. **Cross-Border Payments by Ripple**
   - **Description**: Ripple's blockchain technology enables fast and secure cross-border payments with an immutable transaction record.
   - **Impact**: The immutability of transaction records helps prevent fraud in international payments by ensuring that all transactions are accurately recorded and cannot be altered.

5. **B3i's Insurance Blockchain**
   - **Description**: The Blockchain Insurance Industry Initiative (B3i) uses blockchain to streamline insurance processes and claims.
   - **Impact**: Blockchain's immutability ensures that insurance policies and claims are accurately recorded, reducing the risk of fraudulent claims and ensuring trust between insurers and clients.

Conclusion

The immutability of blockchain technology plays a pivotal role in preventing fraudulent activities in banking and finance. By providing a secure, unalterable, and transparent record of transactions, blockchain helps ensure data integrity, prevent tampering, and reduce the risk of fraud. This characteristic enhances the reliability and trustworthiness of financial systems, making blockchain a valuable tool in combating fraud and maintaining financial security.

9. Blockchain Integration in Existing Systems

Integrating blockchain technology into existing systems can significantly enhance various aspects of operations, from improving transparency and security to streamlining processes and reducing costs.

However, this integration involves overcoming several technical, operational, and strategic challenges. Here's a detailed look at how blockchain can be integrated into existing systems and the key considerations involved:

Key Steps for Blockchain Integration

1. **Assessing Compatibility and Need**

- **Objective**: Evaluate the current system to identify how blockchain can add value and which processes or data can be enhanced by its features.
- **Considerations**: Analyze the existing data flows, security requirements, and transaction processes to determine where blockchain can be most beneficial.

2. **Defining Use Cases and Objectives**
   - **Objective**: Clearly define the specific use cases for blockchain integration and the objectives you aim to achieve.
   - **Considerations**: Choose use cases that benefit from blockchain's immutability, transparency, and decentralization. For example, supply chain tracking, digital identity management, or secure financial transactions.

3. **Choosing the Right Blockchain Type**
   - **Objective**: Select the appropriate blockchain type (public, private, or consortium) based on your use case and requirements.
   - **Considerations**: Public blockchains offer transparency but may have scalability issues. Private blockchains offer better control but may not provide the same level of decentralization.

4. **Integration with Existing Infrastructure**
   - **Objective**: Integrate blockchain technology with current IT systems and applications.
   - **Considerations**:
     - **APIs and Middleware**: Use APIs and middleware to connect blockchain networks with existing systems. This enables data exchange and interaction between blockchain and legacy systems.

- **Data Synchronization**: Ensure that data between blockchain and existing systems is synchronized and consistent.

5. **Developing and Testing Smart Contracts**
   - **Objective**: Develop smart contracts to automate and manage blockchain transactions and processes.
   - **Considerations**: Write, test, and deploy smart contracts carefully to avoid bugs and vulnerabilities. Ensure they interact correctly with existing systems.

6. **Ensuring Data Privacy and Security**
   - **Objective**: Implement security measures to protect sensitive data and comply with privacy regulations.
   - **Considerations**: Encrypt sensitive data on the blockchain and ensure that access controls and permissions are properly configured.

7. **Training and Change Management**
   - **Objective**: Prepare staff and stakeholders for the transition to blockchain-based processes.
   - **Considerations**: Provide training on blockchain technology and its impact on existing workflows. Address any resistance to change and ensure a smooth transition.

8. **Monitoring and Maintenance**
   - **Objective**: Continuously monitor the performance of the blockchain integration and maintain the system.
   - **Considerations**: Implement monitoring tools to track blockchain performance and health. Regularly update and maintain both the blockchain network and integrated systems.

Real-World Examples of Blockchain Integration

1. **Walmart's Supply Chain Management**
    - **Description**: Walmart uses blockchain technology to improve traceability and transparency in its supply chain. By integrating blockchain with its existing supply chain systems, Walmart can track the origin of food products in real time.
    - **Impact**: This integration enhances food safety, reduces fraud, and improves operational efficiency.

2. **J.P. Morgan's Interbank Information Network (IIN)**
    - **Description**: J.P. Morgan has integrated blockchain technology into its existing financial systems through the Interbank Information Network, which facilitates real-time payment and transaction tracking between banks.
    - **Impact**: The blockchain integration improves transaction speed, reduces errors, and enhances transparency in cross-border payments.

3. **De Beers' Tracr Platform**
    - **Description**: De Beers has implemented blockchain to track the provenance of diamonds from mine to market. The Tracr platform integrates with existing diamond trading systems to ensure that all diamonds are conflict-free.
    - **Impact**: Blockchain integration provides an immutable record of each diamond's history, enhancing transparency and reducing the risk of fraud.

4. **Maersk's TradeLens Platform**

- **Description**: Maersk and IBM have developed TradeLens, a blockchain-based platform for global trade. This platform integrates with existing shipping and logistics systems to provide real-time visibility into cargo movements.
- **Impact**: TradeLens improves efficiency, reduces paperwork, and enhances security in global supply chains.

5. **SBI Holdings' Financial Services**
   - **Description**: SBI Holdings, a major Japanese financial group, has integrated blockchain technology into its financial services, including securities trading and payment systems.
   - **Impact**: The integration enhances transaction security, reduces settlement times, and improves overall efficiency.

Conclusion

Integrating blockchain technology into existing systems involves several critical steps, including assessing compatibility, defining use cases, and addressing technical and regulatory challenges. Real-world examples demonstrate that when effectively integrated, blockchain can enhance transparency, security, and efficiency across various sectors. By carefully managing the integration process, organizations can leverage blockchain's capabilities to improve their operations and achieve strategic objectives.

9.1 Challenges of Integration: *Key challenges when integrating blockchain with existing banking and finance systems*

Integrating blockchain technology into existing banking and finance systems presents several challenges. These challenges span technical, operational, regulatory, and strategic dimensions. Addressing these issues is crucial to successfully leveraging blockchain's benefits while mitigating potential risks. Here's a detailed look at the key challenges:

1. Technical Challenges

a. Compatibility with Legacy Systems

- **Issue**: Existing banking and finance systems are often built on legacy technologies that may not be directly compatible with blockchain.
- **Solution**: Implement middleware or APIs to bridge the gap between blockchain and legacy systems. Custom interfaces may be needed to facilitate data exchange and interoperability.

b. Scalability

- **Issue**: Blockchain networks, particularly public ones, can struggle with scalability, impacting transaction speed and throughput.
- **Solution**: Use scalable blockchain platforms or technologies that support high transaction volumes. Explore layer-2 solutions, sidechains, or sharding to improve scalability.

c. Data Synchronization

- **Issue**: Ensuring that data remains synchronized between blockchain and existing systems can be complex.
- **Solution**: Implement robust data integration and synchronization tools. Ensure that data updates on the blockchain are accurately reflected in existing systems.

d. Integration Complexity

- **Issue**: Integrating blockchain technology can be complex and require significant changes to existing processes.
- **Solution**: Develop a detailed integration plan, conduct thorough testing, and use experienced developers to manage the integration process.

2. Operational Challenges

a. Change Management

- **Issue**: Integrating blockchain may require significant changes to existing workflows and processes, leading to resistance from employees.
- **Solution**: Implement a comprehensive change management strategy, including training programs, clear communication, and support for staff during the transition.

b. Training and Skill Development

- **Issue**: Staff may lack the necessary skills and knowledge to work with blockchain technology effectively.
- **Solution**: Invest in training and upskilling programs to ensure that employees are equipped to handle new blockchain-based systems.

c. Cost of Integration

- **Issue**: The financial cost of integrating blockchain technology can be high, including development, implementation, and maintenance costs.
- **Solution**: Conduct a cost-benefit analysis to justify the investment. Explore cost-effective solutions and consider phased implementation to manage expenses.

3. Regulatory and Compliance Challenges

a. Regulatory Uncertainty

- **Issue**: Blockchain technology is subject to evolving regulatory requirements, which can create uncertainty for financial institutions.
- **Solution**: Stay informed about regulatory developments and engage with legal and compliance experts to ensure that blockchain implementations meet current and future regulatory requirements.

b. Data Privacy and Security

- **Issue**: Ensuring compliance with data privacy regulations (such as GDPR) while using blockchain can be challenging due to the immutability and transparency of blockchain data.
- **Solution**: Implement privacy-preserving techniques such as data encryption, zero-knowledge proofs, and selective data sharing to address privacy concerns.

c. Legal Frameworks

- **Issue**: The legal frameworks surrounding blockchain and smart contracts are still developing, which can impact their enforceability and use in financial transactions.
- **Solution**: Work with legal professionals to navigate and influence the development of legal frameworks that support blockchain technology.

4. Strategic and Organizational Challenges

a. Strategic Alignment

- **Issue**: Aligning blockchain integration with overall business strategy and objectives can be challenging.
- **Solution**: Develop a clear strategy for blockchain adoption that aligns with business goals. Ensure that all stakeholders understand and support the strategic vision.

b. Partnership and Collaboration

- **Issue**: Successful blockchain integration often requires collaboration with other organizations, including regulators, technology providers, and industry partners.

- **Solution**: Build strong partnerships and engage in industry consortia to facilitate collaboration and knowledge sharing.

c. Resistance to Change
- **Issue**: There may be resistance to adopting new technologies from various stakeholders, including senior management and employees.
- **Solution**: Foster a culture of innovation and demonstrate the tangible benefits of blockchain integration to overcome resistance.

Real-World Examples of Blockchain Integration Challenges

1. **Deutsche Bank's Blockchain Initiatives**
   - **Challenge**: Deutsche Bank faced challenges integrating blockchain with its existing financial systems due to the complexity and scale of its legacy infrastructure.
   - **Solution**: The bank focused on developing blockchain-based solutions for specific use cases and used APIs to bridge the gap with legacy systems.
2. **JP Morgan's Interbank Information Network (IIN)**
   - **Challenge**: Integrating the IIN with various banks' existing systems required significant coordination and technical adjustments.
   - **Solution**: JP Morgan used a consortium approach, involving multiple banks in the development and integration process to ensure compatibility and address technical issues.
3. **Santander's One Pay FX**
   - **Challenge**: Implementing blockchain technology for international payments involved overcoming regulatory hurdles and

> ensuring compliance with financial regulations.
> - **Solution**: Santander worked closely with regulators and used a private blockchain network to manage cross-border payments while ensuring compliance.
>
> 4. **Maersk's TradeLens**
>   - **Challenge**: Maersk faced challenges integrating TradeLens with existing shipping and logistics systems due to varied legacy technologies used by different stakeholders.
>   - **Solution**: Maersk developed a flexible integration framework and collaborated with industry partners to standardize data formats and improve interoperability.

Conclusion

Integrating blockchain technology with existing banking and finance systems involves navigating technical, operational, regulatory, and strategic challenges. By addressing these challenges proactively and leveraging real-world examples for guidance, financial institutions can successfully integrate blockchain technology to enhance their operations and achieve strategic goals.

9.2 Strategies for Successful Integration: *Best practices for effectively incorporating blockchain into current processes*

Integrating blockchain technology into existing banking and finance processes can bring significant benefits, including enhanced security, transparency, and efficiency. However, successful integration requires careful planning, clear strategies, and adherence to best practices. Here are key strategies to ensure effective incorporation of blockchain technology:

1. Develop a Clear Vision and Strategy

a. Define Objectives

- **Action**: Clearly articulate the goals of blockchain integration. Identify specific problems to address, such as improving transaction speed, reducing fraud, or enhancing transparency.
- **Example**: A bank aiming to streamline cross-border payments might set objectives to reduce transaction costs and processing times through blockchain technology.

b. Align with Business Goals

- **Action**: Ensure that the blockchain strategy aligns with the overall business strategy and objectives. Consider how blockchain can support long-term business goals.
- **Example**: Align blockchain integration with digital transformation initiatives to support a broader vision of modernizing banking operations.

c. Engage Stakeholders

- **Action**: Involve key stakeholders early in the planning process, including management, IT teams, and regulatory bodies, to gain support and ensure alignment.
- **Example**: Conduct workshops and meetings with stakeholders to discuss the benefits and challenges of blockchain integration and gather input.

2. Choose the Right Blockchain Platform

a. Evaluate Platforms

- **Action**: Assess various blockchain platforms based on factors such as scalability, security, compatibility, and support for smart contracts.
- **Example**: Compare platforms like Ethereum, Hyperledger Fabric, and Corda to determine which best fits the needs of your specific application.

b. Consider Private vs. Public Blockchains

- **Action**: Decide between private (permissioned) and public (permissionless) blockchains based on factors such as privacy requirements and the level of control needed.
- **Example**: Use a private blockchain for internal processes that require high confidentiality, while leveraging a public blockchain for transparent transactions.

c. Pilot Projects

- **Action**: Start with pilot projects to test the blockchain solution in a controlled environment before full-scale implementation.
- **Example**: Implement a blockchain-based solution for a specific use case, such as trade finance, to assess its effectiveness and scalability.

3. Focus on Integration and Interoperability

a. Develop Integration Plans

- **Action**: Create a detailed integration plan that outlines how blockchain technology will connect with existing systems and processes.
- **Example**: Use APIs and middleware to integrate blockchain with legacy systems, ensuring smooth data exchange and functionality.

b. Ensure Interoperability

- **Action**: Address interoperability issues by ensuring that the blockchain solution can communicate and work seamlessly with other systems and platforms.
- **Example**: Implement standards and protocols that facilitate interoperability between blockchain networks and traditional financial systems.

c. Use Modular Approaches

- **Action**: Implement blockchain in a modular fashion, allowing for incremental integration and testing of individual components.
- **Example**: Roll out blockchain applications in phases, starting with less critical processes before extending to more complex or mission-critical functions.

4. Address Regulatory and Compliance Requirements

a. Stay Informed

- **Action**: Keep abreast of current and evolving regulations related to blockchain technology and ensure compliance with legal requirements.
- **Example**: Regularly review regulatory updates from authorities such as the Financial Action Task Force (FATF) and local financial regulators.

b. Work with Regulators

- **Action**: Engage with regulatory bodies to understand compliance requirements and influence the development of supportive regulatory frameworks.
- **Example**: Collaborate with regulators during the pilot phase to ensure that the blockchain solution meets regulatory expectations.

c. Implement Privacy and Security Measures

- **Action**: Ensure that blockchain implementations comply with data privacy regulations, such as GDPR, and include robust security measures.

- **Example**: Use encryption and data masking techniques to protect sensitive information while maintaining blockchain transparency.

5. *Invest in Skills and Training*

a. Train Employees
- **Action**: Provide training for employees to build blockchain expertise and ensure they are equipped to work with new technologies.
- **Example**: Conduct workshops and training sessions on blockchain fundamentals, smart contracts, and integration processes.

b. Develop a Center of Excellence
- **Action**: Establish a dedicated team or center of excellence to drive blockchain initiatives and provide ongoing support and expertise.
- **Example**: Create a blockchain innovation lab within the organization to explore new use cases and develop solutions.

c. Foster a Culture of Innovation
- **Action**: Encourage a culture of innovation and experimentation, allowing teams to explore blockchain applications and stay ahead of technological advancements.
- **Example**: Implement hackathons or innovation challenges focused on blockchain to stimulate creative solutions and engagement.

6. *Monitor and Evaluate Performance*

a. Set Key Performance Indicators (KPIs)
- **Action**: Define KPIs to measure the success and impact of blockchain integration, such as transaction speed, cost savings, and user satisfaction.
- **Example**: Track metrics related to transaction processing times and error rates to assess the effectiveness of the blockchain solution.

b. Continuously Improve

- **Action**: Use performance data and feedback to make continuous improvements to the blockchain implementation.
- **Example**: Analyze pilot project results and make necessary adjustments before scaling up the blockchain solution.

c. Stay Updated

- **Action**: Keep up with the latest advancements in blockchain technology and industry best practices to ensure that the solution remains relevant and effective.
- **Example**: Participate in industry conferences and forums to learn about emerging trends and innovations in blockchain.

Real-World Examples

1. **HSBC's Digital Trade Finance**
   o **Challenge**: Integrating blockchain into existing trade finance processes.
   o **Solution**: HSBC launched a blockchain-based digital trade finance platform, integrating with existing systems to enhance transparency and efficiency in trade transactions.
2. **JPMorgan Chase's Interbank Information Network (IIN)**
   o **Challenge**: Integrating IIN with various banks' systems.
   o **Solution**: JPMorgan Chase developed IIN, using blockchain to facilitate cross-border payments while ensuring interoperability with traditional banking systems.
3. **Deutsche Bank's Integration with Digital Ledger Technology**

- **Challenge**: Bridging blockchain with Deutsche Bank's legacy systems.
- **Solution**: Deutsche Bank partnered with fintech firms to test and implement blockchain solutions, focusing on APIs and middleware for integration.

4. **Santander's One Pay FX**
   - **Challenge**: Integrating blockchain for cross-border payments while ensuring regulatory compliance.
   - **Solution**: Santander used a private blockchain network to streamline international payments, integrating with existing payment infrastructure.

By following these strategies and learning from real-world examples, banks and financial institutions can effectively integrate blockchain technology into their existing systems, driving improvements in efficiency, transparency, and security.

9.3 Impact on Legacy Systems: *How blockchain affects and interacts with traditional banking systems*

Blockchain technology introduces transformative changes to traditional banking systems by enhancing transparency, security, and efficiency. However, its integration with legacy systems presents both opportunities and challenges. Understanding the impact of blockchain on traditional banking systems involves examining how blockchain interacts with existing infrastructure, the benefits it offers, and the challenges it poses.

1. Enhancing Transparency and Security

a. Improved Transparency

- **Impact**: Blockchain provides a decentralized ledger that is immutable and transparent, which contrasts with traditional banking systems that often rely on centralized databases with limited visibility.
- **Example**: In a traditional system, transactions are recorded in proprietary ledgers with restricted access. Blockchain allows all participants to view the transaction history, making processes like auditing more straightforward and transparent.

b. Enhanced Security

- **Impact**: The cryptographic principles underpinning blockchain technology offer superior security features compared to traditional systems, which can be vulnerable to hacking and fraud.
- **Example**: Blockchain's use of cryptographic hashing and digital signatures ensures data integrity and prevents tampering. This can significantly reduce the risk of data breaches and fraud in banking operations.

2. Streamlining Processes and Reducing Costs

a. Streamlined Transactions

- **Impact**: Blockchain can streamline transaction processes by eliminating intermediaries and reducing the need for reconciliation. Traditional banking systems often involve multiple intermediaries, each adding time and cost to transactions.
- **Example**: Cross-border payments traditionally involve several banks and clearing houses, leading to delays and high fees. Blockchain can enable direct transactions between parties, reducing processing time and costs.

b. Cost Reduction

- **Impact**: By automating processes and reducing the reliance on intermediaries, blockchain can lower operational costs associated with transaction processing and record-keeping.
- **Example**: Blockchain's smart contracts automate contract execution and compliance, which can reduce administrative costs and errors compared to manual processing.

3. Integration Challenges

a. Compatibility Issues

- **Challenge**: Legacy systems are often built on outdated technology and may not be compatible with blockchain solutions, requiring significant modifications or overhauls.
- **Example**: Integrating blockchain with existing core banking systems may require extensive development work to ensure that data flows seamlessly between blockchain and traditional databases.

b. Data Migration

- **Challenge**: Migrating data from legacy systems to blockchain can be complex and risky, particularly when dealing with large volumes of historical data.
- **Example**: Banks must carefully plan and execute data migration strategies to ensure that historical transaction

records are accurately transferred and synchronized with the blockchain.

c. Integration Costs

- **Challenge**: The cost of integrating blockchain technology with legacy systems can be substantial, including expenses related to technology upgrades, system integration, and staff training.
- **Example**: Banks may face significant upfront costs to implement blockchain solutions, including the expense of hiring specialized personnel and upgrading infrastructure.

4. Regulatory and Compliance Considerations

a. Adapting to Regulations

- **Impact**: Blockchain introduces new regulatory and compliance challenges, as existing regulations may not cover blockchain-specific aspects.
- **Example**: Banks must navigate evolving regulations related to blockchain and digital assets, ensuring that their blockchain implementations comply with legal requirements for data protection, anti-money laundering (AML), and know-your-customer (KYC) practices.

b. Reporting and Auditing

- **Impact**: Blockchain's transparency can enhance auditing and reporting processes, but it also requires new approaches to compliance monitoring and reporting.
- **Example**: Regulators may need to adapt their auditing procedures to account for blockchain's immutable ledger, requiring banks to provide new types of reports and documentation.

5. Opportunities for Innovation

a. New Financial Products and Services

- **Opportunity**: Blockchain enables the creation of innovative financial products and services, such as digital

currencies, tokenized assets, and decentralized finance (DeFi) applications.
- **Example**: Banks can develop new offerings, like blockchain-based asset tokenization platforms or decentralized lending solutions, to attract customers and enhance their competitive edge.

b. Improved Customer Experience
- **Opportunity**: Blockchain can enhance customer experiences by providing faster, more transparent, and secure financial services.
- **Example**: Customers can benefit from real-time transaction tracking and faster cross-border payments, improving overall satisfaction and engagement with banking services.

Real-World Examples

> 1. **JPMorgan Chase's Interbank Information Network (IIN)**
>   - **Impact**: IIN, developed by JPMorgan Chase, uses blockchain to improve the efficiency and transparency of cross-border payments. It interacts with traditional banking systems by integrating with existing payment networks to streamline and expedite transactions.
> 2. **Deutsche Bank's Trade Finance Platform**
>   - **Impact**: Deutsche Bank implemented a blockchain-based trade finance platform to enhance transparency and reduce fraud in trade transactions. The platform integrates with existing trade finance systems, providing a more secure and efficient solution for handling trade documents.
> 3. **BBVA's Blockchain-based Loan Platform**
>   - **Impact**: BBVA used blockchain technology to facilitate syndicated loans, allowing multiple

> banks to participate in loan transactions with greater transparency and efficiency. The blockchain platform integrates with traditional loan processing systems, improving coordination and reducing administrative overhead.
>
> 4. **Santander's Blockchain-based Cross-Border Payments**
>   - **Impact**: Santander's One Pay FX leverages blockchain to provide faster and more transparent international money transfers. The platform integrates with traditional banking infrastructure to enhance the efficiency of cross-border payment processes.

Summary

Blockchain technology significantly impacts traditional banking systems by improving transparency, security, and efficiency. While it offers substantial benefits, such as streamlined transactions and cost reductions, it also presents challenges, including compatibility with legacy systems, data migration, and regulatory compliance. Successful integration requires careful planning, investment in technology and training, and ongoing adaptation to evolving regulatory frameworks. Real-world examples from institutions like JPMorgan Chase, Deutsche Bank, BBVA, and Santander demonstrate how blockchain can be effectively incorporated into existing banking processes, driving innovation and enhancing customer experiences.

10. Future Trends in Blockchain for Finance

As blockchain technology continues to evolve, its impact on the financial sector is expected to deepen, with several emerging trends shaping the future landscape.

These trends promise to transform various aspects of finance, from transaction processing and asset management to regulatory compliance and customer engagement. Here's a look at some key future trends in blockchain for finance:

1. Expansion of Central Bank Digital Currencies (CBDCs)

a. Definition and Development

- **Trend**: Central banks worldwide are exploring and developing Central Bank Digital Currencies (CBDCs) to modernize payment systems and enhance financial inclusion. CBDCs are digital currencies issued and regulated by central banks, leveraging blockchain to ensure security and efficiency.

- **Example**: The People's Bank of China has already begun trials of its digital yuan (e-CNY), aiming to improve the efficiency of the payment system and combat financial crime.

b. Implications for Finance

- **Impact**: CBDCs can streamline payment systems, reduce transaction costs, and offer new monetary policy tools. They also present opportunities for enhanced cross-border payments and financial inclusion, particularly in underbanked regions.

2. Growth of Decentralized Finance (DeFi)

a. Expanding DeFi Ecosystem

- **Trend**: Decentralized Finance (DeFi) continues to grow, with blockchain-based platforms offering a wide range of financial services, including lending, borrowing, trading, and insurance. DeFi eliminates intermediaries and relies on smart contracts to automate financial transactions.

- **Example**: Platforms like Uniswap and Compound are pioneering DeFi services, enabling users to trade cryptocurrencies and earn interest on digital assets without traditional banks.

b. Challenges and Opportunities

- **Impact**: While DeFi offers innovative financial products and greater access to financial services, it also raises regulatory and security challenges. The sector's growth will require addressing these challenges while ensuring robust consumer protection and risk management.

3. Enhanced Blockchain Interoperability

a. Cross-Chain Solutions

- **Trend**: Interoperability between different blockchain networks is becoming increasingly important. Solutions that facilitate seamless interactions across multiple blockchains can enhance the efficiency and flexibility of financial transactions.
- **Example**: Projects like Polkadot and Cosmos aim to create ecosystems where different blockchains can interoperate, allowing for more integrated and versatile financial services.

b. Implications for Financial Systems

- **Impact**: Improved interoperability can lead to more efficient and scalable financial systems, enabling assets and data to move freely across different blockchain platforms and traditional financial systems.

4. Advanced Smart Contract Capabilities

a. Evolving Smart Contracts

- **Trend**: Smart contracts are becoming more sophisticated, with advanced programming capabilities enabling complex financial transactions and automation. Innovations in smart contract technology are expected to drive new financial products and services.
- **Example**: Ethereum 2.0 and other blockchain platforms are enhancing smart contract functionalities, providing more scalability and flexibility for developing financial applications.

b. Impact on Financial Operations

- **Impact**: Enhanced smart contract capabilities can lead to more automated and transparent financial operations, reducing the need for intermediaries and increasing the efficiency of contract execution.

5. Integration of Blockchain with Artificial Intelligence (AI)

a. Synergy between Blockchain and AI

- **Trend**: Combining blockchain with AI technologies can create powerful solutions for fraud detection, risk management, and data analysis. AI can enhance blockchain's capabilities by providing insights and automating decision-making processes.
- **Example**: AI-powered blockchain analytics tools can help financial institutions detect suspicious transactions and predict market trends with greater accuracy.

b. Potential Benefits

- **Impact**: The integration of blockchain and AI can lead to more intelligent and secure financial systems, improving operational efficiency and enhancing decision-making processes.

6. Increased Focus on Privacy and Security

a. Privacy-Enhancing Technologies

- **Trend**: As data privacy concerns grow, there is a rising focus on privacy-enhancing technologies within blockchain systems. Zero-knowledge proofs and other privacy solutions are being developed to protect sensitive financial information while maintaining transparency.
- **Example**: Privacy-focused projects like Zcash and Monero use advanced cryptographic techniques to ensure transaction privacy and security.

b. Implications for Financial Privacy

- **Impact**: Enhanced privacy solutions can address regulatory and consumer concerns about data protection, ensuring that financial transactions remain secure while meeting compliance requirements.

7. Regulatory Evolution and Standards

a. Development of Blockchain Regulations

- **Trend**: As blockchain technology continues to advance, regulatory frameworks will evolve to address emerging challenges and opportunities. Governments and regulatory bodies are working to create standards and guidelines for blockchain use in finance.

- **Example**: The Financial Action Task Force (FATF) has issued guidelines for regulating cryptocurrency exchanges and ensuring compliance with anti-money laundering (AML) and counter-terrorism financing (CTF) requirements.

b. Impact on Financial Institutions

- **Impact**: Evolving regulations will shape the adoption and implementation of blockchain technology in finance, requiring institutions to adapt their strategies and operations to meet new compliance standards.

Real-World Examples

1. **Digital Yuan (e-CNY)**
   - **Description**: China's digital yuan is a Central Bank Digital Currency (CBDC) aimed at modernizing the payment system and enhancing financial inclusion. It is being piloted in various cities and offers insights into the future of CBDCs.

2. **Uniswap**
   - **Description**: Uniswap is a leading decentralized exchange (DEX) that facilitates token swaps without intermediaries. It exemplifies the growth of DeFi and its impact on traditional financial services.

3. **Polkadot**
   - **Description**: Polkadot is a blockchain platform that enables interoperability between different blockchains, allowing for seamless integration and interaction across various decentralized networks.

4. **Zcash**

- **Description**: Zcash is a privacy-focused cryptocurrency that uses zero-knowledge proofs to ensure transaction confidentiality while maintaining the security of the blockchain network.

5. **AI-powered Blockchain Analytics by Chainalysis**
   - **Description**: Chainalysis uses AI and blockchain analytics to provide insights into cryptocurrency transactions, helping financial institutions detect fraud and comply with regulatory requirements.

Summary

The future of blockchain in finance is poised for transformative advancements, including the expansion of CBDCs, the growth of DeFi, enhanced interoperability, advanced smart contract capabilities, and the integration with AI. These trends offer significant opportunities for innovation and efficiency but also present challenges related to privacy, security, and regulatory compliance. Real-world examples from projects like China's digital yuan, Uniswap, Polkadot, Zcash, and Chainalysis illustrate how blockchain is shaping the future of finance, driving progress, and creating new possibilities in the financial sector.

10.1 Emerging Blockchain Technologies: *New and emerging technologies in blockchain that could impact the finance sector*

As blockchain technology evolves, several new and emerging technologies are poised to significantly impact the finance sector. These innovations offer enhanced capabilities, improved efficiency, and new possibilities for transforming financial operations. Here's a detailed look at some of the most promising emerging blockchain technologies and their potential implications for the finance industry:

1. Layer 2 Solutions

a. Definition and Purpose

- **Overview**: Layer 2 solutions are built on top of existing blockchain networks (Layer 1) to improve scalability, reduce transaction fees, and enhance throughput. They address some of the limitations of Layer 1 blockchains, such as high transaction costs and slow processing speeds.
- **Types**: Common Layer 2 solutions include state channels, sidechains, and rollups.
  - **State Channels**: Allow multiple transactions to be conducted off-chain, with only the final result recorded on the main blockchain. This approach enhances transaction speed and reduces fees.
  - **Sidechains**: Independent blockchains connected to the main chain, enabling assets to move between them while processing transactions in parallel.
  - **Rollups**: Bundle multiple transactions into a single batch, reducing the burden on the main blockchain and improving scalability.

b. Examples and Impact

- **Example**: The Lightning Network for Bitcoin and Optimistic Rollups for Ethereum are notable Layer 2 solutions that have significantly improved transaction speed and cost-efficiency.
- **Impact**: Layer 2 solutions can enhance the scalability of blockchain networks, making them more suitable for high-volume financial transactions and applications.

2. Privacy-Enhancing Technologies

a. Overview

- **Definition**: Privacy-enhancing technologies (PETs) aim to provide greater confidentiality and anonymity for transactions on blockchain networks. They address privacy concerns while maintaining the benefits of blockchain's transparency and security.
- **Key Technologies**: Zero-Knowledge Proofs (ZKPs), Confidential Transactions, and Private Smart Contracts.
    - **Zero-Knowledge Proofs**: Cryptographic techniques that allow one party to prove knowledge of a fact without revealing the fact itself. Examples include zk-SNARKs and zk-STARKs.
    - **Confidential Transactions**: Hide the transaction amount while allowing verification of its validity.
    - **Private Smart Contracts**: Enable private execution of smart contracts, ensuring that sensitive data is not exposed on the blockchain.

b. Examples and Impact

- **Example**: Zcash uses zk-SNARKs to provide privacy for cryptocurrency transactions, while the Aztec Protocol offers confidential transactions on Ethereum.
- **Impact**: Privacy-enhancing technologies can address regulatory and consumer concerns about data protection, making blockchain more viable for sensitive financial applications.

3. Decentralized Autonomous Organizations (DAOs)

a. Definition and Function

- **Overview**: DAOs are blockchain-based organizations that are governed by smart contracts and operate without centralized management. They enable decentralized decision-making and resource allocation based on collective stakeholder votes.
- **Features**: DAOs use token-based voting systems to manage governance, funding, and operational decisions. They are often used for community-driven projects and decentralized venture capital.

b. Examples and Impact

- **Example**: The DAO, an early venture capital fund, and MakerDAO, which governs the DAI stablecoin, are prominent examples of DAOs in action.
- **Impact**: DAOs can transform traditional organizational structures by providing decentralized and transparent governance mechanisms, potentially reducing administrative overhead and increasing stakeholder engagement.

4. Cross-Chain Interoperability Solutions

a. Overview

- **Definition**: Cross-chain interoperability solutions enable different blockchain networks to communicate and interact with each other. They facilitate the transfer of assets and data across diverse blockchain platforms.
- **Key Technologies**: Interoperability protocols, cross-chain bridges, and atomic swaps.
  - **Interoperability Protocols**: Frameworks that standardize communication between blockchains, such as Polkadot and Cosmos.

- **Cross-Chain Bridges**: Platforms that allow assets to move between different blockchains, enhancing liquidity and flexibility.
- **Atomic Swaps**: Enable direct peer-to-peer exchange of cryptocurrencies across different blockchains without the need for intermediaries.

b. Examples and Impact

- **Example**: Polkadot's relay chain and Cosmos' Inter-Blockchain Communication (IBC) protocol are key interoperability solutions that enable diverse blockchains to work together.
- **Impact**: Cross-chain interoperability can enhance the utility and integration of blockchain networks, supporting more complex and diverse financial applications.

5. Blockchain-Based Identity Management

a. Definition and Purpose

- **Overview**: Blockchain-based identity management systems use blockchain technology to create secure, decentralized, and verifiable digital identities. These systems can enhance privacy, reduce fraud, and streamline verification processes.
- **Features**: Decentralized identifiers (DIDs), verifiable credentials, and self-sovereign identity (SSI) systems.

b. Examples and Impact

- **Example**: Sovrin is a decentralized identity network that allows users to manage and share their identities securely, while uPort provides a blockchain-based digital identity solution for Ethereum.
- **Impact**: Blockchain-based identity management can improve the security and efficiency of identity verification processes in finance, reducing fraud and enhancing user privacy.

6. Programmable Money and Digital Assets

a. Overview

- **Definition**: Programmable money refers to digital currencies and assets that can be programmed to perform specific functions or behaviors through smart contracts. This concept includes tokenized assets, stablecoins, and programmable financial instruments.
- **Types**: Tokenized assets represent real-world assets like real estate or securities on the blockchain, while stablecoins are designed to maintain a stable value and reduce volatility.

b. Examples and Impact

- **Example**: Tether (USDT) is a widely used stablecoin pegged to the US dollar, while the Real Estate Asset Token (RENT) tokenizes real estate assets for fractional ownership and trading.
- **Impact**: Programmable money and digital assets can revolutionize financial transactions by enabling automated, programmable, and efficient financial instruments.

Real-World Examples

1. **Lightning Network**
    - **Description**: An off-chain Layer 2 solution for Bitcoin that enables faster and cheaper transactions by conducting transactions off the main blockchain.
    - **Impact**: Enhances Bitcoin's scalability and transaction efficiency.
2. **Zcash**
    - **Description**: A cryptocurrency that uses zk-SNARKs to provide privacy for transactions while maintaining blockchain security.

- **Impact**: Addresses privacy concerns in digital currency transactions.

3. **Polkadot**
   - **Description**: A blockchain platform designed for interoperability, allowing different blockchains to communicate and share information.
   - **Impact**: Facilitates cross-chain functionality and integration.

4. **Sovrin**
   - **Description**: A decentralized identity network that provides secure and verifiable digital identities using blockchain technology.
   - **Impact**: Enhances identity security and privacy.

5. **Tether (USDT)**
   - **Description**: A stablecoin pegged to the US dollar, used for stable digital transactions and reducing volatility in the cryptocurrency market.
   - **Impact**: Provides stability in digital asset transactions and trading.

Summary

Emerging blockchain technologies such as Layer 2 solutions, privacy-enhancing technologies, DAOs, cross-chain interoperability, blockchain-based identity management, and programmable money are set to revolutionize the finance sector. These innovations promise to enhance scalability, privacy, and efficiency while introducing new possibilities for financial operations and transactions. Real-world examples demonstrate the practical applications and benefits of these technologies, highlighting their potential to transform the financial landscape.

10.2 Ensuring Security in Blockchain: *Key practices for maintaining security in blockchain systems*

Ensuring security and privacy in blockchain systems is crucial for maintaining the integrity and confidentiality of data while leveraging the benefits of blockchain technology. Here are key practices for maintaining security and privacy in blockchain systems:

1. Implement Strong Cryptographic Practices

Encryption: Use advanced encryption techniques to protect data both at rest and in transit. Cryptographic algorithms like AES (Advanced Encryption Standard) should be employed to secure sensitive information and ensure that only authorized parties can access it.

Hashing: Employ secure hashing algorithms, such as SHA-256 (Secure Hash Algorithm 256-bit), to generate unique cryptographic signatures for data. Hashing ensures data integrity by allowing verification that data has not been altered.

Example: Bitcoin uses SHA-256 hashing to secure transaction data and create new blocks in the blockchain, ensuring the integrity and immutability of the ledger.

2. Adopt Robust Consensus Mechanisms

Proof of Work (PoW) and Proof of Stake (PoS): Choose a consensus mechanism that aligns with your security needs. PoW requires computational effort to validate transactions, while PoS involves staking assets to participate in the validation process. Each has its own security characteristics and trade-offs.

Hybrid Models: Consider hybrid consensus models that combine elements of PoW and PoS to enhance security and achieve a balance between decentralization and efficiency.

Example: Ethereum is transitioning from a PoW to a PoS consensus mechanism with Ethereum 2.0 to improve scalability and energy efficiency while maintaining security.

3. Enhance Network Security

Node Security: Ensure that all nodes in the blockchain network are secured against cyber threats. Implement firewalls, intrusion detection systems, and regular security updates to protect node infrastructure.

Distributed Denial of Service (DDoS) Protection: Deploy DDoS protection mechanisms to safeguard against attacks that aim to overwhelm the network with excessive traffic, disrupting blockchain operations.

Example: Chainlink uses a decentralized network of oracles to provide data to smart contracts, ensuring that the network remains secure and resilient against attacks.

4. Use Privacy-Enhancing Technologies

Zero-Knowledge Proofs: Implement zero-knowledge proofs (ZKPs) to allow parties to verify transactions or claims without revealing the underlying data. ZKPs enhance privacy by ensuring that sensitive information remains confidential.

Confidential Transactions: Utilize confidential transactions techniques to encrypt transaction amounts and other sensitive details, ensuring that only authorized parties can view the information.

Example: Zcash uses zk-SNARKs (zero-knowledge succinct non-interactive arguments of knowledge) to provide privacy for transactions, allowing users to prove the validity of transactions without disclosing details.

5. Implement Smart Contract Security Measures

Code Audits: Conduct thorough audits of smart contract code to identify and fix vulnerabilities before deployment. Engage third-party auditors with expertise in blockchain security to ensure comprehensive reviews.

Testing and Simulation: Test smart contracts in simulated environments to identify potential issues and ensure that they function as intended under various conditions.

Example: OpenZeppelin provides a suite of security tools and services for smart contract audits and testing, helping developers identify and address vulnerabilities in their code.

6. Maintain Secure Identity and Access Controls

Multi-Signature Wallets: Use multi-signature wallets that require multiple private keys to authorize transactions. This adds an additional layer of security by preventing unauthorized access.

Identity Management: Implement secure identity management systems to control and verify access to blockchain resources. Use decentralized identity solutions to enhance privacy and security.

Example: Gnosis Safe offers a multi-signature wallet solution that requires multiple signatures to authorize transactions, enhancing security for managing digital assets.

7. Establish Clear Governance and Compliance Protocols

Governance Framework: Develop a governance framework that outlines roles, responsibilities, and decision-making processes for managing the blockchain network. Ensure that governance practices align with security and privacy goals.

Compliance: Adhere to relevant regulations and standards related to data protection, privacy, and security. Regularly review and update compliance practices to align with evolving legal requirements.

Example: Hyperledger Fabric provides customizable governance models for permissioned blockchains, allowing organizations to define governance structures that meet their security and compliance needs.

8. Educate and Train Stakeholders

Security Awareness: Provide ongoing education and training for stakeholders, including developers, users, and administrators, on best practices for maintaining security and privacy in blockchain systems.

Incident Response: Develop and implement an incident response plan to address potential security breaches or privacy violations.

Ensure that all stakeholders are familiar with the procedures for reporting and responding to incidents.

Example: The Blockchain Training Alliance offers educational resources and training programs focused on blockchain security and best practices, helping organizations build knowledgeable teams.

9. Regularly Monitor and Update Security Measures

Continuous Monitoring: Implement continuous monitoring solutions to detect and respond to potential security threats in real-time. Use tools that provide alerts and insights into network activity and vulnerabilities.

Patch Management: Regularly update and patch blockchain software and infrastructure to address known vulnerabilities and security issues. Stay informed about security updates and apply them promptly.

Example: IBM Security provides solutions for monitoring and managing blockchain security, helping organizations detect and respond to threats in real-time.

In summary, ensuring security and privacy in blockchain systems involves implementing strong cryptographic practices, adopting robust consensus mechanisms, enhancing network security, using privacy-enhancing technologies, securing smart contracts, managing identity and access controls, establishing clear governance and compliance protocols, educating stakeholders, and regularly monitoring and updating security measures. By following these best practices, organizations can maintain the integrity and confidentiality of their blockchain systems while leveraging the technology's benefits.

11. Building Blockchain Knowledge and Skills

As blockchain technology continues to gain prominence across various industries, developing expertise in this area can open up numerous opportunities.

Here's a structured approach to building blockchain knowledge and skills, suitable for both beginners and those looking to deepen their understanding:

1. Fundamental Understanding of Blockchain

a. **Start with Basics**
- **Definition**: Learn what blockchain technology is, including its key concepts such as decentralization, distributed ledgers, and consensus mechanisms.

- **Resources**:
    - **Books**: "Blockchain Basics: A Non-Technical Introduction in 25 Steps" by Daniel Drescher.
    - **Online Courses**: "Blockchain Basics" by the University at Buffalo on Coursera.

b. **Key Concepts**

- **Blocks and Chains**: Understand how data is stored in blocks and linked in a chain.
- **Consensus Mechanisms**: Learn about Proof of Work (PoW), Proof of Stake (PoS), and other consensus algorithms.
- **Cryptography**: Basic principles of cryptographic techniques used in blockchain, such as hashing and digital signatures.

c. **Hands-On Practice**

- **Simulation Tools**: Use platforms like CryptoZombies to get a hands-on introduction to blockchain and smart contracts through interactive coding lessons.

2. Deep Dive into Blockchain Technologies

a. **Explore Blockchain Platforms**

- **Ethereum**: Learn about Ethereum's smart contracts and decentralized applications (dApps).
- **Hyperledger**: Understand the use of Hyperledger Fabric in enterprise solutions.
- **Polkadot**: Explore interoperability and how Polkadot connects different blockchains.

b. **Develop Smart Contracts**

- **Programming Languages**: Study Solidity (for Ethereum) or Chaincode (for Hyperledger).
- **Development Tools**: Use Remix IDE or Truffle Suite for building and testing smart contracts.

c. **Security Considerations**
- **Learn**: About common vulnerabilities and security practices in blockchain development, such as reentrancy attacks and front-running.
- **Resources**: "Smart Contract Security Best Practices" by ConsenSys.

3. Practical Skills and Applications

a. **Build Projects**
- **Create a dApp**: Develop a decentralized application using Ethereum or another blockchain platform.
- **Implement Smart Contracts**: Write and deploy smart contracts on test networks.

b. **Join Blockchain Communities**
- **Forums and Groups**: Participate in blockchain-focused forums like Stack Exchange or join local blockchain meetups and hackathons.

c. **Certifications**
- **Certifications**: Obtain certifications to validate your skills.
  - **Certified Blockchain Developer**: Offered by various institutions like the Blockchain Council.
  - **Certified Blockchain Expert**: Provided by organizations like the Blockchain Certification Institute.

4. Advanced Topics and Trends

a. **Explore Emerging Technologies**
- **Layer 2 Solutions**: Study scalability improvements like Lightning Network and Rollups.
- **Privacy Technologies**: Learn about Zero-Knowledge Proofs and Confidential Transactions.

b. **Stay Updated**

- **Research Papers**: Read recent research and papers to understand cutting-edge developments.
- **Industry Reports**: Review reports and publications from blockchain research firms.

c. **Specialize in Applications**

- **Finance**: Dive into decentralized finance (DeFi) and its impact on traditional banking.
- **Supply Chain**: Explore blockchain's role in tracking and verifying goods in supply chains.

5. Real-World Applications and Case Studies

a. **Case Studies**

- **Financial Sector**: Study blockchain implementations in real-time transactions, fraud detection, and digital currencies.
- **Supply Chain**: Review use cases where blockchain enhances transparency and traceability.

b. **Work on Industry Problems**

- **Identify Problems**: Work on solving real-world problems using blockchain technology, whether through projects or in a professional setting.

c. **Networking and Collaboration**

- **Industry Events**: Attend blockchain conferences and workshops.
- **Collaborations**: Partner with professionals and researchers to work on innovative solutions.

Real-World Examples

1. **IBM Blockchain**
    - **Description**: IBM provides enterprise blockchain solutions using Hyperledger Fabric, focusing on supply chain management and financial services.

- **Impact**: Enhances transparency and efficiency in global supply chains.

2. **Ethereum and Uniswap**
    - **Description**: Ethereum powers decentralized finance (DeFi) platforms like Uniswap, which facilitates automated trading of cryptocurrencies.
    - **Impact**: Revolutionizes financial trading by eliminating intermediaries.

3. **Chainalysis**
    - **Description**: Chainalysis provides blockchain analytics and fraud detection services, helping financial institutions and law enforcement track illicit transactions.
    - **Impact**: Improves security and compliance in the cryptocurrency space.

4. **Polkadot**
    - **Description**: Polkadot enables interoperability between different blockchains, allowing them to communicate and share data.
    - **Impact**: Facilitates a more connected and functional blockchain ecosystem.

5. **Zcash**
    - **Description**: Zcash uses zk-SNARKs to provide privacy-focused cryptocurrency transactions.
    - **Impact**: Addresses privacy concerns while maintaining the security and integrity of transactions.

Summary

Building blockchain knowledge and skills involves understanding fundamental concepts, diving into specific technologies, and gaining practical experience through projects and certifications. By staying updated with emerging trends and engaging in real-world applications, you can develop a comprehensive understanding of blockchain technology and its potential impact on various industries. Real-world examples illustrate how blockchain is being applied in finance, supply chains, and beyond, offering practical insights into its transformative capabilities.

11.1 Educational Resources: *Available resources for learning more about blockchain technology*

As blockchain technology continues to evolve and become more integral across various sectors, numerous educational resources are available to help individuals and professionals deepen their understanding. Here's a comprehensive list of resources categorized by type:

1. Online Courses and Platforms

a. **Coursera**

- **Courses**:
    - "Blockchain Basics" by the University at Buffalo.
    - "Blockchain Specialization" by the University at Buffalo (includes multiple courses covering blockchain fundamentals and applications).
- **Website**: Coursera Blockchain Courses (https://www.coursera.org/)

b. **edX**

- **Courses**:
    - "Blockchain Fundamentals" by the University of California, Berkeley.
    - "Blockchain for Business" by the Linux Foundation.
- **Website**: edX Blockchain Courses (https://www.edx.org/)

c. **Udacity**

- **Nanodegree Programs**:
    - "Blockchain Developer Nanodegree".
    - "Blockchain for Business".

- **Website**: Udacity Blockchain Programs (https://www.udacity.com/)

d. **Pluralsight**
- **Courses**:
  - "Blockchain Fundamentals".
  - "Ethereum and Smart Contracts".
- **Website**: Pluralsight Blockchain Courses (https://www.pluralsight.com/)

e. **LinkedIn Learning**
- **Courses**:
  - "Blockchain Basics".
  - "Learning Blockchain Development with Ethereum".
- **Website**: LinkedIn Learning Blockchain Courses (https://www.linkedin.com/learning)

2. *Websites and Blogs*

a. **CoinDesk**
- **Content**: News, analysis, and educational content on blockchain and cryptocurrencies.
- **Website**: CoinDesk (https://www.coindesk.com/)

b. **Blockchain.com Blog**
- **Content**: Articles and updates on blockchain technology and its applications.
- **Website**: Blockchain.com Blog

c. **The Block**
- **Content**: Industry news and research on blockchain technology.
- **Website**: The Block (https://www.theblock.co/)

d. **Medium (Blockchain Tag)**

- **Content**: A range of articles and opinions from blockchain professionals and enthusiasts.
- **Website**: Medium Blockchain Tag

3. *Research Papers and Journals*

a. **arXiv.org**
- **Papers**: Access research papers on blockchain technology and related topics.
- **Website**: arXiv Blockchain Papers (https://arxiv.org/)

b. **IEEE Xplore**
- **Papers**: Academic papers and conference proceedings on blockchain and its applications.
- **Website**: IEEE Xplore (https://ieeexplore.ieee.org/)

c. **SpringerLink**
- **Papers**: Access research articles and books on blockchain from Springer.
- **Website**: SpringerLink (https://link.springer.com/)

4. *Online Communities and Forums*

a. **Reddit**
- **Subreddits**:
    - r/Bitcoin
    - r/Ethereum
    - r/Blockchain

b. **Stack Exchange**
- **Communities**:
    - Bitcoin Stack Exchange
    - Ethereum Stack Exchange

c. **Telegram Groups**

- **Groups**: Many blockchain-related groups provide discussion, support, and updates.

5. Workshops and Webinars

a. **Blockchain Meetups**

- **Platforms**: Meetups organized via Meetup.com or local blockchain groups.

b. **Conferences**

- **Events**: Attend blockchain conferences such as Consensus, Devcon, and Blockchain Expo.

c. **Webinars**

- **Providers**: Many educational institutions and blockchain organizations offer webinars on specific topics.

6. Interactive Tools

a. **CryptoZombies**

- **Tool**: Interactive coding tutorials for learning smart contracts and Ethereum.
- **Website**: CryptoZombies

b. **Remix IDE**

- **Tool**: Integrated development environment for writing and testing smart contracts in Solidity.
- **Website**: Remix IDE

Summary

Building expertise in blockchain technology involves a combination of theoretical learning and practical experience. Educational resources such as online courses, books, websites, research papers, and interactive tools offer diverse ways to understand and apply blockchain concepts. Engaging with communities, attending conferences, and participating in hands-on projects further enhance learning and skill development in blockchain technology.

12. Real-world case study examples

12.1 Case Study 1: *Implementing Blockchain for Secure Transactions*: The Case of JPMorgan Chase

Introduction

JPMorgan Chase, one of the largest financial institutions in the world, has recognized the transformative potential of blockchain technology in enhancing security and efficiency in financial transactions. This case study explores how JPMorgan has implemented blockchain solutions to secure transactions, streamline processes, and reduce operational risks.

Background

In the traditional banking system, transactions often involve multiple intermediaries, leading to increased costs, delays, and security vulnerabilities. Recognizing these challenges, JPMorgan sought to leverage blockchain technology to improve the security and efficiency of its transaction processes. In 2017, the bank launched **Quorum**, a blockchain platform built on Ethereum, designed specifically for enterprise use.

Objectives

- **Enhance Transaction Security:** Reduce the risk of fraud and errors in financial transactions.
- **Improve Efficiency:** Streamline the transaction process by minimizing the need for intermediaries.
- **Increase Transparency:** Provide a clear, tamper-proof record of transactions.

Implementation

1. **Development of Quorum:**
    - JPMorgan developed Quorum as a permissioned blockchain platform that supports smart contracts and allows for greater privacy in transactions compared to public blockchains. Quorum was

designed to facilitate secure and efficient transactions while maintaining confidentiality.

2. **Integration with Existing Systems:**
   o JPMorgan integrated Quorum with its existing banking systems, allowing for seamless transactions between traditional systems and the blockchain. This integration enabled the bank to utilize blockchain for a variety of applications, including payments, settlements, and trade finance.

3. **Use of Smart Contracts:**
   o Smart contracts on Quorum were deployed to automate transaction processes, ensuring that terms of agreements were executed without the need for manual intervention. This significantly reduced the chances of human error and fraud.

4. **Pilot Projects:**
   o JPMorgan initiated pilot projects to test the capabilities of Quorum in real-world scenarios. One notable pilot was in the area of interbank payments, where the bank collaborated with other financial institutions to facilitate secure and instant cross-border transactions.

Outcomes

1. **Increased Security:**
   o The implementation of Quorum reduced the risk of fraud and errors significantly. With the immutable ledger provided by blockchain, all transaction records were secure and verifiable, enhancing overall trust in the transaction process.

2. **Cost Reduction and Efficiency Gains:**
   o By reducing the need for intermediaries and manual processes, JPMorgan was able to cut costs and improve transaction speeds.

Transactions that previously took days to settle could now be completed in real-time.

3. **Enhanced Transparency:**
   - The transparent nature of blockchain allowed all parties involved in a transaction to access the same data, improving accountability and reducing disputes. This transparency was particularly beneficial in trade finance, where multiple stakeholders are involved.

4. **Regulatory Compliance:**
   - JPMorgan worked closely with regulators to ensure that its blockchain solutions complied with existing financial regulations. This proactive approach helped mitigate regulatory risks and positioned the bank as a leader in blockchain compliance.

Future Directions

Following the success of Quorum, JPMorgan continues to explore further applications of blockchain technology within its operations. The bank is also involved in broader industry collaborations through initiatives like the **Interbank Information Network (IIN)**, which utilizes blockchain to facilitate secure information sharing among banks.

Additionally, JPMorgan is looking to leverage Quorum's capabilities to expand into new areas such as digital identity management and asset tokenization, aiming to further enhance transaction security and efficiency across its services.

Conclusion

JPMorgan Chase's implementation of blockchain technology through its Quorum platform exemplifies how major financial institutions can utilize this innovative technology to secure transactions, improve operational efficiency, and comply with regulatory standards. As blockchain continues to evolve, JPMorgan remains committed to exploring its potential to revolutionize banking and finance.

12.2 Case Study 2: *Smart Contracts in Banking: The Case of BBVA and Its Blockchain-Based Loan Solution*

Introduction

Banco Bilbao Vizcaya Argentaria (BBVA), one of the largest financial institutions in Spain and a leader in digital banking, has embraced blockchain technology to enhance the efficiency and transparency of its operations. This case study focuses on BBVA's implementation of smart contracts for a blockchain-based loan solution, demonstrating how the bank leverages technology to streamline processes and improve customer experiences.

Background

Traditionally, loan agreements involve extensive paperwork, multiple intermediaries, and significant time delays. Recognizing these inefficiencies, BBVA sought to innovate its lending processes by utilizing smart contracts on the Ethereum blockchain. This move aimed to automate and secure the loan issuance and management processes, significantly improving operational efficiency.

Objectives

- **Streamline Loan Processes:** Reduce the time and complexity involved in loan agreements.
- **Enhance Transparency and Trust:** Provide all parties with real-time access to loan information and status updates.
- **Automate Compliance:** Ensure that loan conditions are met automatically through smart contracts.

Implementation

1. **Development of Smart Contracts:**
   - BBVA created a smart contract framework on the Ethereum blockchain to manage loan agreements. The smart contract automates the terms of the

loan, including repayment schedules and interest calculations, removing the need for manual intervention.

2. **Pilot Loan Issuance:**
   - In 2018, BBVA successfully issued a €75 million loan to a Spanish company using its blockchain platform. The loan agreement was executed entirely through the smart contract, which facilitated automatic updates on payment schedules and compliance requirements.

3. **Integration with Existing Systems:**
   - BBVA ensured that its blockchain solution integrated seamlessly with existing banking systems, allowing for smooth interactions between traditional banking processes and the new blockchain framework.

4. **Collaboration with Other Stakeholders:**
   - The bank collaborated with legal teams and regulatory bodies to ensure that the smart contracts met compliance and legal standards, creating a framework that could be used across various financial products.

Outcomes

1. **Increased Efficiency:**
   - The use of smart contracts significantly reduced the time required to issue loans. What typically took weeks or months to finalize was reduced to just a few hours, enhancing the customer experience.

2. **Improved Transparency:**
   - All stakeholders involved in the loan transaction, including borrowers, lenders, and regulatory bodies, could access the same data in real-time.

This transparency helped build trust and reduce disputes related to loan terms and conditions.

3. **Cost Reduction:**
   - By automating various processes, BBVA was able to lower operational costs associated with loan issuance. The reduction in paperwork and manual processing translated to significant cost savings for the bank.

4. **Regulatory Compliance:**
   - BBVA worked closely with regulatory authorities to ensure that the smart contract adhered to relevant financial regulations. This proactive approach minimized regulatory risks and positioned the bank as a pioneer in the use of blockchain in lending.

Future Directions

Following the success of its initial smart contract loan issuance, BBVA plans to expand its use of blockchain technology across other areas of its operations. The bank is exploring the use of smart contracts for other financial products, including mortgages and trade finance. Additionally, BBVA aims to collaborate with other financial institutions to develop industry-wide standards for the use of blockchain and smart contracts.

Conclusion

BBVA's implementation of smart contracts for loan issuance exemplifies how financial institutions can leverage blockchain technology to improve efficiency, transparency, and customer trust. By embracing innovation, BBVA not only enhances its competitive edge but also sets a precedent for other banks in the industry to follow, demonstrating the transformative potential of blockchain in banking and finance.

12.3 Case Study 3: *Revolutionizing Payments and Transfers: The Case of Ripple and Cross-Border Transactions*

Introduction

Ripple, a technology company specializing in real-time gross settlement systems, currency exchange, and remittance networks, has pioneered the use of blockchain technology to enhance payments and transfers in the banking and finance sector. This case study examines how Ripple's blockchain-based solutions, particularly its RippleNet network, have transformed cross-border payments, enabling faster, more secure, and cost-effective transactions.

Background

Cross-border payments have historically been slow, expensive, and fraught with inefficiencies due to reliance on multiple intermediaries and legacy banking systems. Ripple was founded in 2012 with the mission to address these challenges by leveraging blockchain technology to streamline the payment process and enhance liquidity.

Objectives

- **Enhance Speed of Transactions:** Reduce the time taken for cross-border payments from days to seconds.
- **Reduce Costs:** Lower transaction fees associated with international transfers.
- **Increase Transparency:** Provide real-time tracking and visibility of transactions.

Implementation

1. **Development of RippleNet:**
   - RippleNet is a decentralized network that connects banks and financial institutions for seamless cross-border payments. It uses the XRP Ledger, a blockchain protocol that allows for fast and secure transactions.

2. **Partnerships with Financial Institutions:**
   - Ripple has partnered with over 300 financial institutions globally, including Santander, American Express, and PNC, to integrate its payment solutions into their existing systems. These partnerships enable institutions to offer faster and cheaper cross-border payment services to their customers.
3. **Use of XRP as a Bridge Currency:**
   - Ripple introduced XRP, its native digital asset, to facilitate liquidity in cross-border transactions. XRP acts as a bridge currency, allowing for instant conversion between different fiat currencies, reducing the need for pre-funding accounts in destination currencies.
4. **Implementation of On-Demand Liquidity (ODL):**
   - Ripple's On-Demand Liquidity service utilizes XRP to enable real-time cross-border payments without the need for pre-funding. This service allows financial institutions to send and receive payments instantly, improving cash flow and reducing operational costs.

Outcomes

1. **Increased Speed of Transactions:**
   - With RippleNet, cross-border payments can be completed in seconds, compared to traditional systems that can take days. This speed is particularly beneficial for businesses needing to make urgent payments.
2. **Cost Savings:**
   - Financial institutions using RippleNet have reported a significant reduction in transaction fees, often by up to 60%. This cost efficiency is achieved by eliminating intermediaries and streamlining processes.

3. **Improved Customer Experience:**
    - Customers benefit from faster and cheaper transactions, enhancing their overall experience. Businesses, in particular, have found Ripple's services valuable for managing cash flow and reducing the cost of doing business internationally.
4. **Enhanced Transparency:**
    - RippleNet provides real-time tracking of payments, allowing senders and receivers to monitor the status of transactions. This transparency builds trust among users and reduces the potential for disputes.

Future Directions

As Ripple continues to expand its network and services, it is exploring additional use cases for blockchain technology in payments, such as integrating Central Bank Digital Currencies (CBDCs) into its ecosystem. Ripple is also focused on enhancing compliance features to meet the evolving regulatory landscape in various jurisdictions.

Additionally, Ripple aims to strengthen its partnerships with more financial institutions worldwide, facilitating the adoption of blockchain technology in the banking sector and driving further innovations in payments.

Conclusion

Ripple's implementation of blockchain technology for cross-border payments has transformed the way financial institutions conduct international transactions. By leveraging its RippleNet network and the XRP digital asset, Ripple has significantly enhanced the speed, cost-effectiveness, and transparency of cross-border payments. This case study illustrates the potential of blockchain technology to revolutionize banking and finance, paving the way for future innovations in the industry.

12.4 Case Study 4: Transforming Asset Management with Blockchain: *The Case of Fidelity Investments*

Introduction

Fidelity Investments, one of the largest asset management firms in the world, has embraced blockchain technology to innovate and enhance its asset management processes. This case study explores how Fidelity leverages blockchain to improve operational efficiency, transparency, and security in managing investments.

Background

The asset management industry is characterized by complex operations, high costs, and a need for transparency. Traditional systems often involve multiple intermediaries, leading to inefficiencies and increased risk of errors and fraud. In response to these challenges, Fidelity began exploring blockchain technology as a way to streamline its operations and improve client service.

Objectives

- **Enhance Operational Efficiency:** Streamline processes to reduce the time and cost associated with asset management.
- **Improve Transparency:** Provide clients with real-time access to investment data and transaction histories.
- **Increase Security:** Utilize blockchain's inherent security features to protect sensitive financial information.

Implementation

1. **Launch of Fidelity Digital Assets:**
    - In 2018, Fidelity launched Fidelity Digital Assets, a subsidiary aimed at providing custody and trade execution services for digital assets. This initiative included the development of a blockchain infrastructure to manage and track digital assets securely.

2. **Integration of Blockchain for Securities Transactions:**
   - Fidelity has implemented blockchain technology to manage traditional securities transactions. By leveraging blockchain's distributed ledger capabilities, the firm aims to facilitate real-time settlement and improve record-keeping for various asset classes.
3. **Partnerships with Blockchain Innovators:**
   - Fidelity has partnered with several blockchain technology providers and projects, such as Chainalysis for compliance solutions and Blockstream for digital asset custody solutions. These collaborations enhance Fidelity's blockchain capabilities and ensure adherence to regulatory standards.
4. **Pilot Programs and Use Cases:**
   - Fidelity conducted pilot programs to explore the application of blockchain in various asset management scenarios, including tokenization of assets and smart contract integration for automated investment processes.

Outcomes

1. **Increased Efficiency:**
   - By integrating blockchain technology, Fidelity has significantly reduced the time required for asset transactions, moving towards real-time settlement. This efficiency leads to cost savings and improves liquidity for investors.
2. **Enhanced Transparency:**
   - Clients can access real-time information regarding their investments through Fidelity's blockchain-enabled platforms. This transparency fosters greater trust between Fidelity and its clients, as they can track the status of their transactions and holdings at any time.

3. **Improved Security:**
   - The use of blockchain enhances the security of transaction records and client data. The immutable nature of blockchain technology ensures that data cannot be altered without detection, reducing the risk of fraud and cyber threats.
4. **Regulatory Compliance:**
   - Fidelity actively engages with regulators to ensure that its blockchain initiatives comply with existing financial regulations. This proactive approach minimizes legal risks and positions Fidelity as a leader in the responsible adoption of blockchain in asset management.

Future Directions

Fidelity is committed to expanding its blockchain initiatives, exploring further applications such as the tokenization of traditional assets (e.g., real estate, equities) to enhance liquidity and accessibility. The firm is also investigating the use of decentralized finance (DeFi) solutions to provide clients with innovative investment opportunities.

In addition, Fidelity plans to continue collaborating with regulatory bodies to shape a favorable regulatory environment for blockchain-based asset management, ensuring that its solutions remain compliant and secure.

Conclusion

Fidelity Investments' adoption of blockchain technology exemplifies the transformative potential of this innovation in the asset management sector. By enhancing operational efficiency, transparency, and security, Fidelity is setting a benchmark for the industry while ensuring compliance with regulatory standards. This case study highlights the critical role of blockchain in revolutionizing asset management practices and demonstrates how financial institutions can harness technology to better serve their clients.

12.5 Case Study 5: Regulatory Compliance in Banking: *The Case of HSBC and Blockchain*

Introduction

HSBC, one of the world's largest banking and financial services organizations, has recognized the potential of blockchain technology to streamline operations while ensuring compliance with regulatory requirements. This case study examines how HSBC has implemented blockchain solutions to enhance transparency, efficiency, and compliance in its banking operations.

Background

The banking industry faces immense pressure to comply with various regulatory frameworks, including Anti-Money Laundering (AML) and Know Your Customer (KYC) requirements. Traditional systems often involve manual processes that are time-consuming and prone to errors. In 2018, HSBC began exploring blockchain technology as a means to enhance compliance and operational efficiency.

Objectives

- **Enhance Compliance:** Streamline KYC and AML processes to meet regulatory requirements more effectively.
- **Improve Transparency:** Create a clear, immutable record of transactions to facilitate audits and regulatory reporting.
- **Increase Efficiency:** Reduce the time and resources spent on compliance-related tasks.

Implementation

1. **Development of HSBC's Blockchain Strategy:**
    - HSBC partnered with blockchain technology providers to develop a strategic framework for

integrating blockchain into its operations. The focus was on creating a permissioned blockchain network that could securely manage and share compliance-related information.

2. **Launch of the HSBC-Standard Chartered Blockchain Platform:**
    o In 2020, HSBC and Standard Chartered launched a blockchain-based platform for trade finance called **We.Trade**. This platform enables banks to process and share compliance information securely among multiple stakeholders, facilitating cross-border transactions while ensuring adherence to regulatory requirements.

3. **Utilization of Smart Contracts:**
    o HSBC implemented smart contracts within the We.Trade platform to automate compliance checks. These contracts automatically execute predefined conditions, such as verifying that all parties involved have completed their KYC requirements, thereby reducing the risk of human error.

4. **Collaboration with Regulatory Bodies:**
    o HSBC actively engaged with regulatory authorities to ensure that its blockchain solutions met all compliance requirements. The bank worked closely with organizations like the Financial Conduct Authority (FCA) in the UK to address regulatory concerns and shape a conducive environment for blockchain adoption.

Outcomes

1. **Improved Compliance Efficiency:**
    o By automating KYC and AML processes through blockchain technology, HSBC has significantly reduced the time required for compliance checks.

Tasks that previously took weeks can now be completed in a matter of days.

2. **Enhanced Transparency and Trust:**
    - The use of an immutable blockchain ledger provides regulators and stakeholders with a clear view of transaction histories. This transparency helps build trust with clients and regulatory bodies, as they can access verified information in real-time.

3. **Cost Savings:**
    - The efficiency gained from blockchain integration has resulted in cost savings for HSBC. By reducing the manual workload associated with compliance, the bank can allocate resources more effectively and minimize operational costs.

4. **Strengthened Regulatory Relationships:**
    - HSBC's proactive approach in collaborating with regulatory authorities has positioned the bank as a leader in compliance within the blockchain space. This engagement has facilitated a smoother rollout of blockchain solutions, as regulatory concerns have been addressed early in the development process.

Future Directions

HSBC plans to continue exploring the use of blockchain technology to further enhance compliance and operational efficiencies. The bank is investigating additional applications of blockchain in areas such as cross-border payments and trade finance, with the goal of expanding its blockchain-based services.

Additionally, HSBC aims to collaborate with other financial institutions and regulatory bodies to establish industry standards for blockchain compliance, ensuring that its solutions not only meet current regulatory requirements but also adapt to future changes in the regulatory landscape.

Conclusion

HSBC's implementation of blockchain technology for regulatory compliance showcases the transformative potential of this innovation in the banking sector. By enhancing compliance efficiency, improving transparency, and building trust with regulators, HSBC is setting a benchmark for the industry. This case study highlights the critical role of blockchain in meeting regulatory challenges and demonstrates how financial institutions can leverage technology to navigate the complexities of compliance in banking and finance.

12.6 Case Study 6: *Combating Fraud in Banking:* The Case of Santander and Blockchain Technology

Introduction

Santander Group, one of the largest banks in Europe, has been at the forefront of implementing innovative technologies to enhance its banking services. Recognizing the increasing threat of fraud in the financial sector, Santander has integrated blockchain technology into its operations to bolster fraud prevention measures. This case study examines how Santander uses blockchain to enhance security, reduce fraud, and improve customer trust.

Background

Fraud in banking is a significant issue, costing the financial industry billions each year. Traditional systems often struggle to detect and prevent fraudulent activities due to the reliance on outdated technologies and manual processes. To address these challenges, Santander initiated a project to explore how blockchain could provide a more secure and efficient solution.

Objectives

- **Enhance Fraud Detection:** Utilize blockchain's immutable ledger to track transactions and detect fraudulent activities more effectively.
- **Improve Security:** Ensure secure transaction records to protect against tampering and unauthorized access.
- **Increase Customer Trust:** Build confidence among customers through enhanced security measures.

Implementation

1. **Partnership with Distributed Ledger Technology (DLT) Providers:**
   - Santander partnered with several blockchain technology firms to develop a proprietary DLT solution aimed at preventing fraud. This

partnership enabled the bank to leverage advanced blockchain capabilities tailored to its specific needs.

2. **Launch of the Santander One Pay FX App:**
   - In 2018, Santander launched the **One Pay FX** app, which utilizes blockchain technology for real-time international money transfers. The app leverages blockchain's transparency and immutability to ensure secure and tamper-proof transaction records.

3. **Implementation of Smart Contracts:**
   - The bank integrated smart contracts within its blockchain framework to automate compliance checks and transaction validations. These contracts can automatically flag suspicious activities based on pre-defined criteria, enhancing fraud detection capabilities.

4. **Real-time Monitoring and Analytics:**
   - Santander employed advanced analytics tools to monitor transactions on the blockchain in real-time. This capability allows for immediate detection of anomalies that could indicate fraudulent activity, enabling swift intervention.

Outcomes

1. **Reduced Fraud Incidents:**
   - Since implementing blockchain technology, Santander has reported a significant decrease in fraudulent transactions. The transparency and traceability of blockchain transactions have made it much more difficult for fraudsters to manipulate records.

2. **Enhanced Security Posture:**
   - The use of an immutable ledger has strengthened the bank's security measures. Transaction records cannot be altered once confirmed, reducing the

risk of fraud and increasing the integrity of the banking system.

3. **Increased Customer Trust:**
    - Customers have responded positively to the enhanced security measures. The transparency provided by blockchain technology has improved customer confidence in the safety of their transactions.

4. **Operational Efficiency:**
    - The integration of smart contracts and real-time monitoring has streamlined Santander's fraud prevention processes. The automation of compliance checks and fraud alerts has reduced manual workload and allowed the bank to allocate resources more effectively.

Future Directions

Santander is committed to further developing its blockchain capabilities to enhance fraud prevention and improve other banking operations. The bank plans to explore additional applications of blockchain technology, such as expanding its use in trade finance and lending.

Furthermore, Santander aims to collaborate with industry stakeholders and regulators to develop standardized protocols for blockchain-based fraud prevention measures, setting benchmarks for security practices across the financial sector.

Conclusion

Santander's implementation of blockchain technology for fraud prevention illustrates the significant potential of this innovation in enhancing security in banking. By improving fraud detection, increasing transaction security, and building customer trust, Santander has positioned itself as a leader in adopting cutting-edge technologies to combat fraud. This case study underscores the critical role of blockchain in addressing the evolving challenges of fraud in the banking and finance industry.

12.7 Case Study 7: *Integrating Blockchain into Existing Systems: The Case of JPMorgan Chase*

Introduction

JPMorgan Chase, one of the largest and most influential financial institutions globally, has been exploring blockchain technology to enhance its operations and service offerings. This case study examines how JPMorgan Chase has successfully integrated blockchain into its existing banking systems, focusing on their Interbank Information Network (IIN) and the implications for efficiency, transparency, and customer service.

Background

Traditional banking systems face numerous challenges, including slow transaction times, high operational costs, and complex compliance requirements. The need for a more efficient and transparent solution led JPMorgan Chase to explore blockchain technology, recognizing its potential to streamline processes and improve collaboration among banks.

Objectives

- **Enhance Transaction Speed:** Reduce the time taken for cross-border payments and interbank transactions.
- **Improve Transparency:** Provide real-time visibility into transactions for all parties involved.
- **Facilitate Compliance:** Streamline the process of meeting regulatory requirements and reduce the burden on back-office operations.

Implementation

1. **Development of the Interbank Information Network (IIN):**
    - In 2017, JPMorgan Chase launched the **IIN**, a blockchain-based platform designed to improve the speed and efficiency of interbank

transactions. The IIN connects participating banks through a shared ledger, allowing for real-time communication and transaction tracking.

2. **Use of Quorum Blockchain:**
    - JPMorgan developed **Quorum**, a permissioned blockchain platform built on Ethereum, to power the IIN. Quorum supports smart contracts and offers enhanced privacy features, enabling banks to share sensitive information securely while maintaining compliance.

3. **Integration with Existing Banking Systems:**
    - JPMorgan worked to seamlessly integrate IIN with its existing payment processing systems and infrastructure. This integration ensured that the benefits of blockchain could be realized without overhauling the entire banking system.

4. **Collaboration with Other Banks:**
    - JPMorgan actively engaged with other financial institutions to encourage participation in the IIN. By building a collaborative network, JPMorgan aimed to create a critical mass of users that would enhance the platform's effectiveness and appeal.

Outcomes

1. **Increased Transaction Speed:**
    - The IIN has significantly reduced the time required for cross-border payments. Transactions that previously took several days can now be completed in real-time, enhancing the overall efficiency of the banking process.

2. **Enhanced Transparency:**
    - The shared ledger allows all participating banks to track transactions in real-time, improving visibility and reducing the potential for errors.

This transparency fosters trust among banks and enhances the security of transactions.

3. **Reduced Operational Costs:**
   - By streamlining the interbank transaction process, JPMorgan has reported a decrease in operational costs associated with cross-border payments. The automation of many compliance tasks has further contributed to cost savings.

4. **Facilitated Regulatory Compliance:**
   - The blockchain platform provides built-in features that help banks comply with regulatory requirements more easily. The ability to access a real-time, tamper-proof transaction history simplifies the audit process and reduces compliance risks.

Future Directions

JPMorgan plans to continue expanding the IIN, exploring additional applications for blockchain technology within the bank's operations. Future enhancements may include the integration of more financial products and services, as well as expanding the network to include additional banks globally.

Furthermore, JPMorgan is investing in research and development to explore how blockchain can improve other aspects of banking, such as trade finance and asset management.

Conclusion

JPMorgan Chase's integration of blockchain technology into its existing systems through the Interbank Information Network demonstrates the significant benefits that blockchain can offer to the banking industry. By enhancing transaction speed, improving transparency, and facilitating compliance, JPMorgan is leading the way in adopting innovative solutions that address the evolving needs of the financial sector. This case study illustrates the potential for blockchain to transform banking operations and highlights the importance of strategic integration in realizing its benefits.

12.8 Case Study 8: *Future Trends in Blockchain for Finance: The Case of Wells Fargo and its Blockchain Innovations*

Introduction

Wells Fargo, a leading financial services company in the United States, has embraced blockchain technology as part of its strategic vision to enhance efficiency, security, and innovation within the financial sector. This case study explores how Wells Fargo is positioning itself to capitalize on future trends in blockchain, examining specific initiatives that demonstrate its commitment to leveraging this transformative technology.

Background

The financial services industry is undergoing significant changes driven by advancements in technology, regulatory pressures, and evolving customer expectations. Blockchain, with its promise of transparency, security, and efficiency, presents an opportunity for banks to rethink traditional processes and create new value propositions. Wells Fargo recognized these trends early on and initiated several projects to explore blockchain's potential.

Objectives

- **Enhance Transaction Efficiency:** Leverage blockchain to streamline processes, reduce transaction times, and lower costs.
- **Improve Security and Trust:** Utilize the inherent security features of blockchain to protect sensitive financial data and build customer trust.
- **Explore New Financial Products:** Innovate by creating new services and products enabled by blockchain technology.

Implementation

1. **Collaboration on the Marco Polo Network:**

- Wells Fargo has partnered with other banks and technology firms to participate in the **Marco Polo Network**, a blockchain-based platform focused on trade finance. This initiative aims to enhance cross-border payments and supply chain finance through improved visibility and efficiency.

2. **Integration of the Wells Fargo Digital Cash System:**
    - In 2020, Wells Fargo introduced its **Digital Cash** system, which uses blockchain technology to facilitate instant interbank transactions. This system allows for the secure transfer of funds between its branches and subsidiaries, significantly reducing the time and costs associated with traditional methods.

3. **Exploring Central Bank Digital Currencies (CBDCs):**
    - Wells Fargo is actively researching the implications of CBDCs and their potential impact on the banking ecosystem. The bank is engaging with regulatory bodies and other financial institutions to understand how CBDCs could be integrated into existing systems and the broader implications for monetary policy.

4. **Investment in Blockchain Startups:**
    - To stay at the forefront of blockchain innovations, Wells Fargo has invested in various blockchain startups and initiatives. This strategy not only enhances its technology stack but also provides insights into emerging trends and applications in the blockchain space.

Outcomes

1. **Increased Transaction Speed and Efficiency:**
    - The implementation of the Digital Cash system has resulted in near-instantaneous transfers between Wells Fargo's entities, significantly

improving operational efficiency and reducing the need for manual reconciliation.

2. **Enhanced Security Measures:**
    - The use of blockchain technology has strengthened security protocols, ensuring that transaction data is tamper-proof and accessible only to authorized parties. This has increased customer confidence in the bank's ability to protect their financial information.

3. **Innovative Financial Solutions:**
    - By participating in the Marco Polo Network, Wells Fargo has been able to offer its clients enhanced trade finance solutions that leverage real-time data and blockchain's transparency. This innovation provides a competitive edge in the trade finance market.

4. **Thought Leadership in CBDCs:**
    - Wells Fargo's research and engagement with CBDC initiatives position the bank as a thought leader in the discussion surrounding digital currencies, enabling it to influence policy and best practices in this emerging area.

Future Directions

Wells Fargo plans to expand its blockchain initiatives by further integrating blockchain technology into other areas of its operations, including consumer banking and wealth management. The bank is also exploring partnerships with fintech firms to accelerate the development of innovative blockchain solutions.

Moreover, as the regulatory landscape for blockchain and digital currencies evolves, Wells Fargo aims to play an active role in shaping policies that foster innovation while ensuring compliance and security.

Conclusion

Wells Fargo's proactive approach to embracing blockchain technology exemplifies how traditional financial institutions can leverage emerging trends to drive innovation and enhance customer service. By investing in blockchain initiatives, collaborating with industry partners, and exploring the future of digital currencies, Wells Fargo is positioning itself as a leader in the financial sector's transformation. This case study illustrates the significant potential of blockchain to reshape banking practices and the importance of strategic foresight in navigating future trends.

12.9 Case Study 9: *Enhancing Security and Privacy with Blockchain:* The Case of Bank of America

Introduction

Bank of America (BoA) is one of the largest financial institutions in the United States, providing a wide range of banking and financial services to millions of customers. As cyber threats continue to evolve, the bank has recognized the need to adopt advanced technologies to enhance security and privacy. This case study explores how Bank of America is utilizing blockchain technology to bolster its security framework, protect customer data, and ensure compliance with regulatory requirements.

Background

With the rise of digital banking, financial institutions face increasing threats from cybercriminals. Traditional security measures often fall short against sophisticated attacks, necessitating innovative solutions. Bank of America has been at the forefront of exploring blockchain technology as a means to enhance security protocols, particularly in transaction verification and data integrity.

Objectives

- **Enhance Data Security:** Utilize blockchain's immutable ledger to protect sensitive financial information from unauthorized access and tampering.
- **Ensure Privacy Compliance:** Develop solutions that comply with privacy regulations, such as GDPR and CCPA, while maintaining customer trust.
- **Streamline Verification Processes:** Improve transaction verification and authentication processes to reduce fraud and enhance operational efficiency.

Implementation

1. **Development of a Blockchain-Based Secure Transactions Platform:**

- Bank of America initiated the development of a proprietary blockchain platform aimed at securing financial transactions. This platform leverages the decentralized nature of blockchain to create a tamper-proof record of all transactions, enhancing security and transparency.

2. **Smart Contracts for Automated Compliance:**
   - The bank integrated smart contracts into its blockchain solution to automate compliance checks for various regulations. These contracts automatically execute predefined actions when conditions are met, significantly reducing the manual oversight required and minimizing human error.

3. **Collaboration with Regulatory Bodies:**
   - To ensure compliance with data protection regulations, Bank of America has engaged with regulators to understand the implications of blockchain technology on privacy. The bank has worked to develop solutions that meet regulatory standards while maximizing the benefits of blockchain.

4. **Employee Training and Knowledge Building:**
   - Bank of America invested in training programs to build blockchain knowledge and skills among its employees. This initiative included workshops, webinars, and partnerships with educational institutions to foster a culture of innovation and ensure staff are well-versed in the implications of blockchain for security and privacy.

Outcomes

1. **Improved Data Integrity:**
   - The implementation of blockchain technology has resulted in a more secure and tamper-resistant data management system. This ensures that

transaction records are accurate and trustworthy, reducing the risk of fraud.

2. **Enhanced Privacy Compliance:**
    o By using smart contracts for compliance automation, Bank of America has streamlined its processes for adhering to privacy regulations. This proactive approach has positioned the bank favorably in the eyes of regulators and customers alike.

3. **Reduced Operational Costs:**
    o The automation of compliance checks and transaction verification has led to significant cost savings by reducing the need for extensive manual oversight and minimizing processing times.

4. **Increased Employee Competence:**
    o The training programs have successfully equipped employees with the necessary skills and knowledge to leverage blockchain technology effectively, fostering an innovative mindset throughout the organization.

Future Directions

Bank of America plans to further enhance its blockchain initiatives by exploring additional applications in areas such as customer identity verification and secure document management. The bank aims to expand its blockchain capabilities to improve not only security and privacy but also overall customer experience.

Moreover, Bank of America is keen on collaborating with other financial institutions and technology partners to develop industry standards for blockchain security, ensuring that best practices are shared and implemented across the sector.

Conclusion

Bank of America's commitment to leveraging blockchain technology highlights the potential for innovation in enhancing security and privacy in the banking sector. By implementing a blockchain-based secure transactions platform and focusing on employee training, the bank is positioning itself as a leader in adopting cutting-edge solutions to address evolving security challenges. This case study illustrates the transformative impact of blockchain technology on financial security and the importance of proactive measures in safeguarding customer information.

12.10 Case Study 10: *Empowering Employees Through Blockchain Education*: The Case of HSBC

Introduction

HSBC, one of the largest banking and financial services organizations in the world, has recognized the transformative potential of blockchain technology within the banking sector. To harness this potential, HSBC has invested in building blockchain knowledge and skills among its employees. This case study explores HSBC's initiatives to educate its workforce on blockchain technology and its applications, focusing on how this investment is driving innovation and enhancing competitive advantage.

Background

The rapid evolution of technology in finance, particularly blockchain, has created a pressing need for banks to upskill their employees. HSBC identified a knowledge gap regarding blockchain's fundamentals and its practical applications in banking and finance. To remain competitive, the bank aimed to equip its staff with the necessary skills to leverage blockchain technology effectively.

Objectives

- **Increase Understanding of Blockchain Technology:** Provide employees with a comprehensive understanding of blockchain concepts, principles, and applications in finance.

- **Foster Innovation:** Encourage a culture of innovation by enabling employees to explore new use cases for blockchain technology within the organization.

- **Enhance Competitive Advantage:** Position HSBC as a leader in blockchain adoption in the banking sector by having a knowledgeable workforce capable of implementing blockchain solutions.

Implementation

1. **Development of a Comprehensive Training Program:**
    - HSBC developed a structured training program on blockchain fundamentals, which includes online courses, in-person workshops, and hands-on labs. The program covers essential topics such as distributed ledger technology, smart contracts, and consensus mechanisms.

2. **Partnerships with Educational Institutions:**
    - HSBC partnered with renowned universities and blockchain experts to create specialized courses and certifications. These collaborations helped ensure that the training materials were up-to-date with industry standards and best practices.

3. **Internal Blockchain Innovation Labs:**
    - The bank established **Blockchain Innovation Labs** where employees could experiment with blockchain applications in a controlled environment. These labs provide resources and tools for teams to develop prototypes and explore real-world use cases.

4. **Knowledge Sharing and Community Building:**
    - HSBC launched an internal platform for employees to share insights, discuss ideas, and collaborate on blockchain-related projects. This community-building initiative fosters engagement and knowledge exchange among staff from different departments.

Outcomes

1. **Increased Blockchain Literacy:**
    - A significant number of employees have completed the blockchain training program, resulting in a marked increase in overall blockchain literacy within the organization. This

knowledge enables staff to better understand the implications of blockchain for their specific roles.

2. **Enhanced Innovation and Collaboration:**
    - The creation of Blockchain Innovation Labs has led to several successful prototypes and projects, including applications in trade finance and cross-border payments. Teams are collaborating across departments, driving innovation throughout the organization.

3. **Strengthened Competitive Position:**
    - By investing in employee education and innovation, HSBC has positioned itself as a forward-thinking leader in the banking sector. This strategic focus on blockchain knowledge has enhanced the bank's reputation as a technology-driven financial institution.

4. **Employee Engagement and Satisfaction:**
    - Employees report increased job satisfaction and engagement, driven by the opportunity to learn new skills and contribute to innovative projects. This investment in their development has created a more motivated workforce.

Future Directions

HSBC plans to expand its blockchain education initiatives by introducing advanced training modules and certifications for employees seeking to deepen their expertise. The bank is also looking to integrate blockchain training into its leadership development programs to ensure that executives are equipped to make informed decisions regarding blockchain investments.

Furthermore, HSBC aims to establish collaborations with fintech startups to explore emerging blockchain solutions and stay ahead of industry trends, ensuring that its workforce remains at the cutting edge of technology in finance.

Conclusion

HSBC's commitment to building blockchain knowledge and skills among its employees underscores the importance of education in harnessing the full potential of emerging technologies. By investing in comprehensive training programs, fostering innovation through dedicated labs, and creating a collaborative knowledge-sharing environment, HSBC is empowering its workforce to lead the charge in blockchain adoption. This case study illustrates how investing in employee education not only enhances individual capabilities but also drives organizational innovation and competitive advantage in the rapidly evolving banking landscape.

12.11 Case Study 11: The Future of Finance: *How Santander is Utilizing Blockchain for Cross-Border Transfers*

Introduction

Santander, one of the world's largest banks, has recognized the transformative potential of blockchain technology in enhancing the efficiency of cross-border transfers. This case study explores Santander's implementation of blockchain for international payments, focusing on the innovations brought about by this technology and its impact on operational efficiency and customer experience.

Company Overview

Santander, headquartered in Spain, serves millions of customers worldwide. With a long history in banking, Santander has been proactive in exploring digital innovations to improve its services. The bank's commitment to integrating blockchain technology into its operations has positioned it as a leader in the financial sector.

Problem Statement

Traditional cross-border payment systems are often slow, costly, and involve multiple intermediaries, resulting in high fees and long wait times for customers. Santander aimed to address these challenges by leveraging blockchain technology to streamline international money transfers and enhance customer satisfaction.

Blockchain Application: One Pay FX

Santander developed **One Pay FX**, a blockchain-based international payments service that utilizes distributed ledger technology to facilitate fast and secure cross-border transfers. Key features of this application include:

1. **Real-Time Transfers**: One Pay FX enables instant international payments, allowing customers to send money across borders in real-time, a significant improvement over traditional systems that can take days to process.

2. **Lower Costs**: By reducing the number of intermediaries involved in cross-border transactions, Santander has lowered transaction fees, making it more cost-effective for customers to send money internationally.
3. **Transparency and Security**: The use of blockchain ensures that all transactions are recorded on an immutable ledger, enhancing the security and transparency of the payment process. Customers can track their payments in real-time, increasing trust in the system.
4. **Ease of Use**: One Pay FX is integrated into Santander's existing mobile banking app, providing a seamless user experience for customers. Users can initiate transfers directly from their smartphones, making international payments as simple as domestic transactions.

Implementation

- **Pilot Launch**: Santander launched One Pay FX in 2018 as a pilot program in several countries, including Spain, the UK, and Poland, focusing on remittances and small-to-medium business payments.
- **Partnerships**: The bank partnered with Ripple, a leading blockchain technology provider, to implement the underlying technology for One Pay FX. This collaboration allowed Santander to leverage Ripple's existing network for enhanced transaction efficiency.
- **Customer Education**: To ensure customer buy-in, Santander conducted educational campaigns to inform users about the benefits of One Pay FX, addressing concerns about security and usability.

Outcomes

1. **Increased Transaction Speed**: One Pay FX has reduced the average time for cross-border payments from several days to mere seconds, significantly enhancing customer satisfaction.

2. **Cost Savings for Customers**: Transaction fees have been reduced by up to 80% compared to traditional methods, making international transfers more accessible.

3. **Wider Adoption**: Following the successful pilot, Santander expanded the service to additional countries, continually increasing its user base and transaction volume.

4. **Strengthened Market Position**: Santander's innovative use of blockchain technology has positioned the bank as a leader in the financial sector, enhancing its reputation for adopting cutting-edge technologies.

Future Directions

Santander plans to further enhance One Pay FX by integrating additional features, such as cryptocurrency capabilities and smart contracts for more complex transactions. The bank is also exploring partnerships with other financial institutions to broaden the reach of its blockchain payment services.

Conclusion

Santander's implementation of blockchain technology through One Pay FX demonstrates the significant advantages of using blockchain for cross-border transfers. The combination of real-time payments, reduced costs, enhanced security, and user-friendly access has positioned Santander as a pioneer in the banking sector's digital transformation. This case study illustrates how embracing blockchain not only improves operational efficiency but also enhances customer experience and trust in financial services.

12.12 Case Study 12: Revolutionizing Payment Processing: *The Case of Visa and Blockchain Integration*

Introduction

Visa, a global leader in digital payments, has recognized the potential of blockchain technology to enhance payment processing efficiency and security. This case study examines Visa's initiatives to integrate blockchain into its operations, exploring the implications for transaction speed, cost reduction, and overall service improvement.

Company Overview

Visa Inc. is one of the largest electronic payment networks in the world, facilitating millions of transactions daily across the globe. As a pioneer in payment solutions, Visa continuously seeks innovative technologies to improve the customer experience and streamline operations.

Problem Statement

Traditional payment processing systems often face challenges related to transaction speed, high fees, and the complexities of cross-border payments. Visa identified these pain points and sought to leverage blockchain technology to create a more efficient and cost-effective payment solution.

Blockchain Application: Visa B2B Connect

Visa developed **Visa B2B Connect**, a blockchain-based platform designed specifically for cross-border business-to-business (B2B) payments. Key features of the platform include:

1. **Instant Settlements**: Visa B2B Connect allows for near-instantaneous settlement of cross-border transactions, significantly reducing the time taken compared to traditional systems that can take several days.

2. **Lower Costs**: By eliminating the need for multiple intermediaries in the payment process, Visa B2B Connect

reduces transaction costs, providing businesses with a more economical solution for international payments.

3. **Enhanced Security**: The platform utilizes blockchain's cryptographic principles to ensure secure and transparent transactions. Each transaction is recorded on an immutable ledger, reducing the risk of fraud and enhancing trust.
4. **Transparency and Tracking**: Users can track their payments in real time, enhancing visibility and allowing businesses to manage cash flows more effectively.

Implementation

- **Pilot Program**: Visa launched a pilot program for Visa B2B Connect in 2019, collaborating with select financial institutions and corporations to test the platform's capabilities in real-world scenarios.
- **Partnerships with Banks**: Visa partnered with banks and fintech companies to expand its network and facilitate smooth integrations of the blockchain platform into existing banking systems.
- **Stakeholder Engagement**: The company engaged with stakeholders to gather feedback and refine the platform, ensuring it met the needs of businesses and financial institutions alike.

Outcomes

1. **Increased Efficiency**: Visa B2B Connect has reduced transaction times from days to mere hours, greatly enhancing operational efficiency for businesses engaged in international trade.
2. **Cost Reductions**: Businesses utilizing the platform have reported transaction cost reductions of up to 30%, significantly improving their bottom line for cross-border payments.
3. **Wider Adoption**: Following the successful pilot, Visa has expanded the platform's availability, with numerous

banks and corporations now utilizing Visa B2B Connect for their international payment needs.

4. **Strengthened Market Position**: Visa's integration of blockchain technology has solidified its position as an innovator in the payment processing industry, attracting new clients and enhancing its reputation as a technology-forward financial service provider.

Future Directions

Visa plans to expand the capabilities of Visa B2B Connect by incorporating additional features such as support for digital currencies and enhanced smart contract functionalities to automate and streamline transactions further. The company is also exploring opportunities to integrate the platform with emerging fintech solutions to enhance interoperability.

Conclusion

Visa's adoption of blockchain technology through the Visa B2B Connect platform exemplifies the significant advantages that blockchain can bring to payment processing. By leveraging blockchain's capabilities, Visa has improved transaction speed, reduced costs, and enhanced security, thereby revolutionizing the cross-border payments landscape. This case study illustrates how the strategic integration of blockchain technology can drive innovation and enhance competitive advantage in the rapidly evolving financial sector.

12.13 Case Study 13: Blockchain vs. Traditional Databases: *Key Differences Explored Through the Case of IBM*

Introduction

IBM, a pioneer in technological innovation, has explored the differences between blockchain technology and traditional databases, recognizing the unique advantages and challenges that each presents. This case study investigates how IBM has leveraged these differences to enhance its services and improve business operations, particularly in sectors like supply chain management and finance.

Company Overview

IBM Corporation is a global technology and consulting company with a diverse range of services, including cloud computing, AI, and blockchain solutions. Known for its focus on research and development, IBM has positioned itself as a leader in enterprise-level blockchain technology through its **IBM Blockchain** platform.

Background

Traditional databases, while effective for many applications, often struggle with issues related to data integrity, security, and transparency. In contrast, blockchain technology offers decentralized, immutable, and secure transaction records. IBM aimed to analyze these differences and apply blockchain solutions to real-world problems, particularly in industries requiring high levels of trust and traceability.

Key Differences Between Blockchain and Traditional Databases

1. **Data Structure**:
    - **Traditional Database**: Data is organized in tables, and transactions are processed in a centralized manner, leading to potential data inconsistencies.
    - **Blockchain**: Data is stored in blocks linked in a chain, ensuring that all transactions are

chronologically recorded and immutable once confirmed.

2. **Control and Accessibility**:
   - **Traditional Database**: Controlled by a single entity, making it vulnerable to manipulation and centralized points of failure.
   - **Blockchain**: Distributed across a network of nodes, providing transparency and reducing the risk of single-point failures.

3. **Security**:
   - **Traditional Database**: Relies on conventional security measures, which can be vulnerable to breaches.
   - **Blockchain**: Utilizes cryptographic techniques to secure data, making it resistant to tampering and fraud.

4. **Cost and Speed**:
   - **Traditional Database**: Can incur high costs and delays due to multiple intermediaries in transaction processes.
   - **Blockchain**: Reduces costs and speeds up transaction processing by eliminating intermediaries and providing real-time settlement.

Implementation

- **IBM Food Trust**: One of IBM's flagship blockchain projects, IBM Food Trust uses blockchain to enhance transparency and traceability in the food supply chain. This platform allows stakeholders, from farmers to retailers, to track the journey of food products in real time, improving safety and reducing waste.
- **Partnerships with Retail Giants**: IBM collaborated with companies like Walmart and Nestlé to implement blockchain solutions. These partnerships highlighted how

blockchain can ensure food safety and enhance trust in the supply chain.

Outcomes

1. **Increased Transparency**: Participants in the IBM Food Trust network have reported significant improvements in visibility throughout the supply chain, allowing for quicker response times to food safety issues.
2. **Enhanced Traceability**: The ability to trace food products back to their source has reduced the time taken to identify contaminated products, improving consumer safety and trust.
3. **Operational Efficiency**: Companies using IBM's blockchain solutions have experienced reduced operational costs and improved efficiency, with some reporting savings of up to 30% in supply chain costs.
4. **Strengthened Market Position**: By integrating blockchain technology, IBM has positioned itself as a leader in enterprise blockchain solutions, attracting new clients across various sectors.

Future Directions

IBM aims to continue exploring the potential of blockchain beyond supply chain management, including applications in finance, healthcare, and identity verification. The company is also committed to developing tools that enhance the interoperability of blockchain networks, facilitating broader adoption across industries.

Conclusion

IBM's exploration of the differences between blockchain technology and traditional databases illustrates the transformative potential of blockchain in various sectors. By leveraging the unique advantages of blockchain, IBM has enhanced transparency, efficiency, and trust in its services. This case study highlights the importance of understanding the fundamental differences between these technologies to harness their full potential in addressing complex business challenges.

12.14 Case Study 14: *Blockchain's Role in Banking: The Case of JPMorgan Chase*

Introduction

JPMorgan Chase, one of the largest and most influential financial institutions in the world, has recognized the transformative potential of blockchain technology in the banking sector. This case study explores how JPMorgan has integrated blockchain solutions into its services, focusing on specific applications, benefits, and the strategic advantages gained from adopting this technology.

Company Overview

JPMorgan Chase & Co. is a multinational investment bank and financial services holding company, offering a wide range of services including investment banking, financial services for consumers and businesses, and asset management. The firm has been at the forefront of adopting innovative technologies to enhance its services and streamline operations.

Background

As the financial industry evolves, traditional banking systems face challenges such as inefficiencies, high transaction costs, and issues related to security and transparency. Recognizing these challenges, JPMorgan began exploring blockchain technology to improve its operations and client services.

Key Applications of Blockchain in Banking

1. **Payments and Settlements**:
    - **JPM Coin**: In 2019, JPMorgan launched JPM Coin, a digital currency designed for facilitating instantaneous payments between institutional clients. This initiative allows for secure and efficient transactions, significantly reducing the time and costs associated with traditional cross-border payments.
2. **Smart Contracts**:

- JPMorgan has been experimenting with smart contracts on blockchain platforms to automate and streamline various financial processes. This includes automating the settlement of trades, thereby minimizing human error and increasing operational efficiency.

3. **Trade Finance**:
    - Through the **Blockchain Trade Finance** platform, JPMorgan has streamlined documentation processes related to trade finance. By using blockchain to create a secure and transparent ledger of transactions, the bank has reduced fraud risk and improved transaction times.

4. **Identity Verification**:
    - Blockchain technology is being leveraged to enhance Know Your Customer (KYC) processes. By maintaining a secure and immutable record of customer identities, JPMorgan can streamline compliance while reducing the time and costs associated with KYC checks.

Implementation

- **Partnerships and Collaborations**: JPMorgan has collaborated with various fintech companies and consortia, such as the **Enterprise Ethereum Alliance** and **R3**, to develop and implement blockchain solutions that meet industry standards and regulatory requirements.
- **In-House Development**: The bank has invested in its own blockchain development team, focusing on building proprietary solutions that address specific needs within its operations.

Outcomes

1. **Enhanced Efficiency**: The implementation of JPM Coin has led to reduced transaction times from days to seconds

for interbank transfers, significantly enhancing operational efficiency.

2. **Cost Reduction**: Automating processes through smart contracts has decreased operational costs associated with traditional banking operations, including labor and transaction fees.

3. **Improved Security and Transparency**: By utilizing blockchain for trade finance and KYC processes, JPMorgan has enhanced the security of transactions and reduced the likelihood of fraud.

4. **Market Leadership**: By being an early adopter of blockchain technology, JPMorgan has positioned itself as a leader in the banking sector, attracting clients interested in innovative financial solutions.

Future Directions

JPMorgan plans to expand its blockchain initiatives by:

- Exploring additional applications in other areas such as asset management and derivatives.
- Enhancing the capabilities of JPM Coin to facilitate more complex transactions and expand its use among a broader range of clients.
- Continuing to advocate for regulatory clarity in blockchain and cryptocurrency, ensuring compliance while fostering innovation.

Conclusion

JPMorgan Chase's strategic integration of blockchain technology demonstrates its commitment to innovation in the banking sector. By leveraging blockchain for payments, smart contracts, trade finance, and identity verification, the bank has improved efficiency, reduced costs, and enhanced security. This case study illustrates how forward-thinking financial institutions can harness blockchain technology to drive operational improvements and maintain a competitive edge in a rapidly evolving marketplace.

12.15 Case Study 15: Decentralization: *How Decentralization Impacts Traditional Banking Systems — The Case of BBVA*

Introduction

Banco Bilbao Vizcaya Argentaria (BBVA), a prominent multinational financial services company based in Spain, has embraced the concept of decentralization through blockchain technology. This case study explores how BBVA has implemented decentralized solutions, the implications for traditional banking systems, and the transformative potential of blockchain in creating a more efficient and transparent financial ecosystem.

Company Overview

BBVA is a leading financial institution that offers a wide range of services, including retail banking, corporate banking, and wealth management. The bank has consistently been at the forefront of adopting innovative technologies to enhance its offerings and improve customer experiences.

Background

Traditional banking systems rely heavily on centralized models, leading to challenges such as inefficiencies, high operational costs, and limited access to financial services. In response to these challenges, BBVA recognized the need for a more decentralized approach, leveraging blockchain technology to enhance its services.

Key Impacts of Decentralization in Banking

1. **Enhanced Efficiency in Transactions**:
    - BBVA has implemented blockchain for international money transfers, significantly reducing transaction times from days to minutes. This decentralization eliminates the need for intermediary banks, streamlining the process and reducing costs.
2. **Increased Transparency and Trust**:

- By utilizing blockchain's distributed ledger technology, BBVA provides clients with real-time visibility into their transactions. This transparency fosters trust among customers, as they can verify transaction details without relying on third-party intermediaries.

3. **Access to Financial Services**:
   - Decentralization allows BBVA to reach underserved populations who may not have access to traditional banking. Through blockchain, the bank can offer microloans and digital identity solutions, enabling financial inclusion for individuals in remote areas.

4. **Smart Contracts for Automation**:
   - BBVA has started to implement smart contracts to automate various banking processes, such as loan agreements and trade finance transactions. This automation reduces the need for manual intervention, minimizing errors and accelerating processing times.

Implementation

- **Blockchain Pilots**: BBVA launched pilot projects to explore the application of blockchain technology in various banking functions. One notable project involved the issuance of a blockchain-based loan, demonstrating the practical applications of decentralized finance.
- **Partnerships and Collaborations**: The bank has collaborated with technology firms and blockchain consortia, such as **R3** and **Hyperledger**, to develop and implement decentralized solutions that align with industry standards.

Outcomes

1. **Cost Savings**:
   - By reducing transaction costs and increasing efficiency, BBVA has realized significant

savings, which can be passed on to customers in the form of lower fees and better rates.

2. **Improved Customer Experience**:
   - The introduction of decentralized services has enhanced the overall customer experience, with faster transactions and greater transparency leading to higher customer satisfaction.

3. **Strengthened Market Position**:
   - BBVA's early adoption of blockchain technology has positioned it as a leader in the banking sector, attracting tech-savvy customers and investors interested in innovative financial solutions.

4. **Increased Financial Inclusion**:
   - The bank's efforts to reach underserved populations have resulted in a broader customer base, contributing to BBVA's growth and social impact.

Future Directions

BBVA plans to further expand its decentralized initiatives by:

- Developing additional blockchain-based products and services, such as decentralized finance (DeFi) offerings.
- Enhancing collaborations with fintech startups to innovate and integrate emerging technologies.
- Investing in research and development to explore new use cases for blockchain across different banking functions.

Conclusion

BBVA's embrace of decentralization through blockchain technology illustrates the significant impacts on traditional banking systems. By enhancing efficiency, transparency, and accessibility, the bank has not only improved its operations but also strengthened its position in a competitive marketplace. This case study highlights how decentralization can transform the banking sector, fostering innovation and driving positive change in financial services.

12.16 Case Study 16: How Blockchain Secures Transactions: *Mechanisms That Ensure Transaction Security and Integrity — The Case of Ripple*

Introduction

Ripple, a technology company specializing in real-time gross settlement systems, currency exchange, and remittance networks, has emerged as a leader in utilizing blockchain technology to secure financial transactions. This case study explores the mechanisms Ripple employs to ensure transaction security and integrity, highlighting how these mechanisms differentiate Ripple from traditional payment systems.

Company Overview

Founded in 2012, Ripple aims to revolutionize cross-border payments by enabling secure, instant, and low-cost international transactions. Its blockchain-based platform, RippleNet, facilitates transactions between different currencies and financial institutions, making it a key player in the financial technology landscape.

Background

Traditional banking systems often face challenges related to transaction security, speed, and transparency. With the advent of blockchain technology, Ripple identified an opportunity to enhance the security and efficiency of cross-border transactions. By leveraging blockchain, Ripple aims to address these challenges while providing a trustworthy platform for financial institutions.

Mechanisms of Transaction Security in Ripple

1. **Decentralized Consensus Protocol**:
    - Ripple employs a unique consensus algorithm known as the Ripple Protocol Consensus Algorithm (RPCA). Instead of relying on a central authority, transactions are validated

through a network of independent validators. This decentralization ensures that no single entity has control over the transaction process, reducing the risk of fraud.

2. **Cryptographic Security**:
   o Each transaction on RippleNet is secured using cryptographic techniques. Transactions are hashed, creating a unique identifier that is difficult to tamper with. The use of public and private keys ensures that only authorized users can initiate transactions, maintaining data integrity.

3. **Real-Time Settlement**:
   o Ripple's technology allows for real-time settlement of transactions, significantly reducing the time required for cross-border payments. By ensuring that transactions are confirmed and settled instantly, Ripple minimizes the risk of errors or fraudulent activities associated with prolonged settlement times.

4. **Immutable Ledger**:
   o Ripple utilizes a distributed ledger that is immutable, meaning that once a transaction is recorded, it cannot be altered or deleted. This feature prevents fraud and enhances transparency, as all participants can view the transaction history.

5. **Multi-signature Transactions**:
   o Ripple supports multi-signature functionality, which requires multiple parties to sign off on a transaction before it can be executed. This added layer of security ensures that transactions are authorized by multiple stakeholders, further reducing the likelihood of unauthorized access.

6. **Transaction Monitoring and Alerts**:

- Ripple employs advanced monitoring tools to track transactions in real-time. Any suspicious activities trigger alerts, allowing for immediate investigation and action. This proactive approach to security helps prevent potential fraud before it occurs.

Implementation at Ripple

Ripple has successfully integrated these security mechanisms into its platform, resulting in widespread adoption among banks and financial institutions. By facilitating secure cross-border transactions, Ripple has positioned itself as a trusted solution for global payments.

Outcomes

1. **Increased Adoption by Financial Institutions**:
    - The robust security features of RippleNet have attracted numerous banks and payment providers, enhancing trust in the platform. Institutions like Santander and American Express have adopted Ripple's technology for their cross-border payment solutions.

2. **Reduction in Fraudulent Activities**:
    - The implementation of decentralized consensus and cryptographic techniques has led to a significant decrease in fraud incidents compared to traditional banking methods, where centralized systems are more vulnerable to attacks.

3. **Enhanced Transaction Speed**:
    - Ripple's real-time settlement capabilities have improved transaction speeds from days to seconds, providing a competitive edge in the fast-paced world of international finance.

4. **Improved Transparency**:
    - The immutable ledger allows for complete transparency in transaction history, fostering trust

among participants and stakeholders involved in cross-border payments.

Future Directions

Ripple plans to continue enhancing its security mechanisms by:

- Developing advanced machine learning algorithms for better transaction monitoring and fraud detection.
- Expanding partnerships with additional financial institutions to increase the network's robustness and reach.
- Exploring interoperability with other blockchain networks to enhance its transaction capabilities across different platforms.

Conclusion

Ripple's innovative use of blockchain technology demonstrates how robust security mechanisms can transform the landscape of financial transactions. By leveraging decentralized consensus, cryptographic security, and real-time settlement, Ripple has set a new standard for transaction integrity and security in the financial sector. This case study illustrates the effectiveness of blockchain in addressing the challenges faced by traditional payment systems, paving the way for a more secure and efficient global payment ecosystem.

12.17 Case Study 17: Cryptographic Principles in Blockchain: *Securing Data with IBM's Hyperledger Fabric*

Introduction

IBM, a global leader in technology and consulting, has been at the forefront of developing blockchain solutions that utilize cryptographic principles to secure data. This case study explores how IBM's Hyperledger Fabric employs advanced cryptographic techniques to ensure the security, integrity, and confidentiality of transactions on its blockchain platform.

Company Overview

IBM launched Hyperledger Fabric as part of the Hyperledger Project in 2016, aiming to provide an open-source framework for enterprise-grade blockchain applications. Designed for scalability and flexibility, Hyperledger Fabric supports various industries, including finance, supply chain, and healthcare, by enabling secure and transparent transactions.

Background

The increasing reliance on digital transactions has necessitated robust security measures to protect sensitive data from cyber threats. IBM recognized the importance of cryptography in blockchain technology to enhance data security. Hyperledger Fabric integrates advanced cryptographic techniques to provide a secure environment for enterprises.

Cryptographic Techniques in Hyperledger Fabric

1. **Public and Private Key Infrastructure**:
    - Hyperledger Fabric employs a public and private key infrastructure (PKI) to manage user identities and transactions. Each participant in the network has a unique digital identity represented by a cryptographic key pair. This ensures that only authorized users can initiate or validate transactions.

2. **Digital Signatures**:
   - Each transaction in Hyperledger Fabric is accompanied by a digital signature created using the sender's private key. This signature verifies the authenticity of the transaction and ensures that it has not been altered during transmission. The corresponding public key can be used by any participant to confirm the signature's validity.

3. **Hash Functions**:
   - Hyperledger Fabric utilizes secure hash functions (such as SHA-256) to create a unique hash for each transaction. Hashing ensures data integrity by providing a fixed-size output that represents variable-sized input data. Any changes to the transaction data result in a different hash, indicating tampering.

4. **Encryption of Data**:
   - Data stored on Hyperledger Fabric can be encrypted both at rest and in transit. This encryption ensures that sensitive information remains confidential and can only be accessed by authorized participants with the appropriate decryption keys.

5. **Consensus Mechanisms**:
   - Hyperledger Fabric employs a modular consensus mechanism, allowing organizations to select the most suitable approach for their needs. This flexibility enhances security by enabling different methods for validating transactions, including crash fault tolerance and Byzantine fault tolerance.

6. **Chaincode and Smart Contracts**:
   - Hyperledger Fabric supports smart contracts, known as chaincode, which are executed in a secure environment. These contracts are

cryptographically signed and can enforce rules and business logic, ensuring that only valid transactions are processed.

Implementation in Hyperledger Fabric

IBM has successfully implemented these cryptographic principles in Hyperledger Fabric, resulting in a robust framework that meets the security needs of various industries. Organizations can customize their security protocols to align with their specific requirements, making Hyperledger Fabric a versatile solution.

Outcomes

1. **Enhanced Security**:
   - The integration of advanced cryptographic techniques has significantly enhanced the security of transactions on Hyperledger Fabric. Organizations using the platform report a reduction in fraud and data breaches compared to traditional systems.

2. **Increased Trust Among Participants**:
   - The use of digital signatures and public key infrastructure fosters trust among network participants, as they can verify the authenticity of transactions and the identity of counterparties.

3. **Regulatory Compliance**:
   - Hyperledger Fabric's cryptographic features assist organizations in complying with industry regulations that mandate strict data protection and privacy measures, making it suitable for highly regulated sectors such as finance and healthcare.

4. **Scalability and Flexibility**:
   - The modular design of Hyperledger Fabric, combined with its cryptographic capabilities, allows organizations to scale their blockchain solutions while maintaining security, enabling them to adapt to changing business needs.

Future Directions

IBM plans to continue enhancing Hyperledger Fabric by:

- Developing more sophisticated cryptographic algorithms to counter emerging cyber threats.

- Expanding the platform's interoperability with other blockchain solutions to facilitate seamless transactions across networks.

- Enhancing user training programs to promote best practices in cryptographic security among developers and enterprises.

Conclusion

IBM's Hyperledger Fabric exemplifies how cryptographic principles can be effectively integrated into blockchain technology to secure data and enhance transaction integrity. By leveraging digital signatures, encryption, and robust consensus mechanisms, Hyperledger Fabric provides a secure framework for enterprises to conduct business in a transparent and trustworthy manner. This case study highlights the critical role of cryptography in the evolution of blockchain solutions, ensuring that organizations can confidently navigate the digital landscape.

12.18 Case Study 18: Revolutionizing Financial Transactions: *The Power of Smart Contracts at ChainSafe Systems*

Introduction

ChainSafe Systems, a leading blockchain development company, has harnessed the capabilities of smart contracts to enhance the efficiency and security of financial transactions. This case study explores how ChainSafe Systems implemented smart contracts in its solutions to streamline operations, reduce costs, and improve trust among stakeholders in various financial applications.

Company Overview

Founded in 2017, ChainSafe Systems specializes in building decentralized applications (dApps) and providing blockchain consulting services. With expertise in Ethereum and other blockchain platforms, ChainSafe aims to drive innovation in finance, gaming, and data privacy through blockchain technology.

Background

The traditional financial system often involves intermediaries, lengthy processes, and high costs, leading to inefficiencies and potential errors. Recognizing these challenges, ChainSafe sought to leverage smart contracts to automate and secure transactions, thereby reducing reliance on intermediaries and enhancing transparency.

Understanding Smart Contracts

Smart contracts are self-executing contracts with the terms of the agreement directly written into code on a blockchain. They automatically enforce and execute contractual obligations when predetermined conditions are met. This automation reduces the need for third-party intermediaries, minimizing costs and errors.

Implementation of Smart Contracts at ChainSafe Systems

1. **Development of Smart Contract Solutions**:

- ChainSafe created customizable smart contract templates for various financial applications, such as lending, insurance, and escrow services. These templates allow clients to quickly deploy smart contracts tailored to their specific needs.

2. **Integration with Existing Systems**:
    - The company worked closely with clients to integrate smart contracts into their existing financial systems. This involved building APIs that facilitate seamless communication between traditional databases and blockchain networks.

3. **Automated Compliance and Reporting**:
    - Smart contracts include built-in compliance features that automatically execute actions based on regulatory requirements. This automation simplifies reporting processes, ensuring that organizations remain compliant without manual intervention.

4. **Real-Time Auditing and Transparency**:
    - By deploying smart contracts on a public blockchain, ChainSafe enabled real-time auditing capabilities. Stakeholders can access transaction records and audit trails, enhancing trust and transparency.

5. **User Education and Training**:
    - ChainSafe provided comprehensive training sessions for clients to ensure they understood the benefits and functionalities of smart contracts. This educational initiative empowered users to leverage the technology effectively.

Outcomes

1. **Increased Efficiency**:
    - The implementation of smart contracts significantly reduced transaction processing

times, with some operations completed in seconds rather than days. This efficiency has improved overall productivity for clients.

2. **Cost Reduction**:
    o By minimizing the need for intermediaries and automating processes, clients reported substantial cost savings. This reduction in operational expenses has made financial services more accessible.

3. **Enhanced Security and Trust**:
    o The cryptographic nature of smart contracts ensures that transactions are secure and tamper-proof. Clients experienced a decrease in fraud incidents, bolstering trust among stakeholders.

4. **Greater Flexibility and Customization**:
    o The ability to create customized smart contracts allowed clients to address unique business challenges and adapt quickly to market changes, enhancing their competitive edge.

Case Study Example: A Lending Platform

One notable project involved a decentralized lending platform built using ChainSafe's smart contract templates. The platform allowed borrowers to secure loans without the need for traditional credit checks. Instead, the smart contract evaluated collateral and executed loan agreements automatically, resulting in quicker approvals and reduced costs for both lenders and borrowers.

Future Directions

ChainSafe plans to enhance its smart contract offerings by:

- Developing advanced features such as dynamic contracts that can adapt to changing conditions and market variables.

- Expanding partnerships with financial institutions to explore new applications for smart contracts in areas like asset tokenization and cross-border payments.
- Investing in research and development to stay ahead of technological advancements and regulatory changes.

Conclusion

ChainSafe Systems exemplifies how smart contracts can revolutionize financial transactions by automating processes, enhancing security, and fostering trust among stakeholders. By implementing these innovative solutions, ChainSafe has not only improved operational efficiency for its clients but has also contributed to the broader adoption of blockchain technology in the financial sector. This case study highlights the transformative potential of smart contracts and their role in shaping the future of finance.

12.19 Case Study 19: Transforming Cross-Border Transfers: *The Case of RippleNet*

Introduction

Ripple Labs Inc., the company behind RippleNet, has emerged as a game-changer in the financial industry by utilizing blockchain technology to facilitate international money transfers. This case study explores Ripple's innovative approach to cross-border payments, highlighting the advantages of its blockchain-based system in enhancing speed, cost-effectiveness, and transparency.

Company Overview

Founded in 2012, Ripple is a technology company specializing in payment solutions. RippleNet, its global payment network, enables financial institutions to process cross-border transactions efficiently using blockchain technology and its native digital currency, XRP.

Background

Traditional cross-border payment systems are often slow, costly, and plagued by a lack of transparency. Transactions can take several days to settle, and high fees are charged at multiple stages. Recognizing these challenges, Ripple sought to revolutionize the international payment landscape by developing a blockchain-based solution that addresses these inefficiencies.

Objectives

- **Increase Speed of Transactions**: Enable real-time or near-real-time settlement of cross-border payments.
- **Reduce Costs**: Minimize transaction fees associated with international money transfers.
- **Enhance Transparency**: Provide stakeholders with clear visibility into the transaction process.

Implementation of RippleNet

1. **Blockchain Technology Adoption**:

- RippleNet utilizes a distributed ledger technology (DLT) that enables secure, instant transactions across borders. The blockchain eliminates the need for intermediaries, streamlining the payment process.

2. **XRP as a Bridge Currency**:
   - Ripple introduced XRP, a digital asset that acts as a bridge currency in transactions. This allows for instant conversion between different fiat currencies, significantly reducing the time and costs involved.

3. **Integration with Financial Institutions**:
   - Ripple has partnered with over 300 financial institutions worldwide, enabling seamless integration of its technology into existing payment infrastructures. This collaboration allows banks and payment providers to offer improved services to their customers.

4. **Liquidity Solutions**:
   - Ripple provides on-demand liquidity solutions, allowing financial institutions to source liquidity without holding pre-funded accounts in destination currencies. This further accelerates the settlement process and reduces operational costs.

5. **Real-Time Monitoring and Reporting**:
   - RippleNet includes features for real-time tracking and reporting of transactions, enhancing transparency and allowing users to monitor their payments throughout the process.

Outcomes

1. **Accelerated Transaction Speed**:
   - Transactions on RippleNet are completed in seconds, compared to traditional systems that

may take several days. This speed is particularly beneficial for businesses requiring fast payments.

2. **Cost Savings**:
   - Ripple's model significantly reduces the costs associated with cross-border payments. Financial institutions report savings of up to 60% in transaction fees compared to traditional payment methods.

3. **Enhanced Transparency**:
   - Stakeholders benefit from a transparent payment process, with the ability to track transactions in real-time. This transparency fosters trust among users and reduces disputes.

4. **Wider Adoption and Market Penetration**:
   - Ripple's partnerships with major financial institutions have led to widespread adoption of its technology, positioning RippleNet as a leading solution in the cross-border payments market.

Case Study Example: A Partnership with Santander

One notable collaboration involved Santander Bank, which integrated Ripple's technology into its One Pay FX service. This service enables customers to make cross-border payments instantly and at lower costs, showcasing the practical benefits of RippleNet in real-world applications.

Future Directions

Ripple aims to continue expanding its global reach and enhancing its technology by:

- Exploring additional use cases for blockchain in finance, such as trade finance and asset tokenization.
- Developing new features that enhance user experience and operational efficiency.

- Collaborating with regulatory bodies to ensure compliance and foster a supportive regulatory environment for blockchain technology.

Conclusion

RippleNet represents a significant advancement in cross-border payment solutions, demonstrating the transformative power of blockchain technology. By addressing the inefficiencies of traditional payment systems, Ripple has not only enhanced transaction speed and reduced costs but also fostered greater transparency in international transfers. This case study illustrates how blockchain can redefine financial services and improve the global payments landscape.

12.20 Case Study 20: Digital Currencies and Their Role in Blockchain-Based Payments: *The Case of JPMorgan Chase*

Introduction

JPMorgan Chase, one of the largest financial institutions globally, has embraced digital currencies as part of its strategy to enhance payment systems. This case study examines how JPMorgan has integrated digital currencies into its operations, particularly through its own digital currency, JPM Coin, and its implications for blockchain-based payments.

Company Overview

Founded in 2000, JPMorgan Chase is a multinational investment bank and financial services holding company. With a strong focus on innovation, it continually seeks to leverage technology to improve its financial services and offer new solutions to clients.

Background

The rise of digital currencies has transformed the landscape of payments, prompting financial institutions to explore blockchain technology. Traditional payment systems often involve lengthy processing times and high fees, making digital currencies an appealing alternative. Recognizing this trend, JPMorgan sought to develop a proprietary digital currency to enhance transaction efficiency.

Objectives

- **Streamline Payment Processes**: Reduce the time and cost associated with cross-border payments.
- **Enhance Client Services**: Offer innovative payment solutions to institutional clients.
- **Leverage Blockchain Technology**: Utilize blockchain's transparency and security features to build trust in digital transactions.

Implementation of JPM Coin

1. **Development of JPM Coin**:
   - Launched in 2020, JPM Coin is a digital currency designed for instantaneous transfers of value between institutional clients. It operates on a private blockchain, providing a secure environment for transactions.

2. **Integration with Existing Systems**:
   - JPMorgan integrated JPM Coin into its existing payment platforms, allowing clients to use the digital currency for real-time settlements. This integration was crucial for providing a seamless user experience.

3. **Partnerships with Corporate Clients**:
   - The bank actively partnered with corporations to encourage the use of JPM Coin for various transactions, such as cross-border payments and supply chain financing. This collaboration helps showcase the benefits of digital currencies in real-world applications.

4. **Regulatory Compliance**:
   - JPMorgan worked closely with regulators to ensure that JPM Coin complied with existing financial regulations, addressing concerns about digital currencies and maintaining trust with clients.

5. **Educational Initiatives**:
   - The bank launched educational programs for clients to help them understand the benefits and uses of digital currencies. This initiative aimed to facilitate adoption among businesses unfamiliar with blockchain technology.

Outcomes

1. **Faster Transactions**:
   - Transactions using JPM Coin can be completed in seconds, significantly reducing the time taken for cross-border payments compared to traditional methods, which can take days.

2. **Cost Efficiency**:
   - The use of JPM Coin has led to reduced transaction fees for clients, making it a more attractive option for large-scale transfers and settlements.

3. **Increased Adoption**:
   - JPMorgan has reported growing interest and participation from corporate clients, with several major companies beginning to use JPM Coin for their transactions.

4. **Enhanced Transparency and Security**:
   - The blockchain-based nature of JPM Coin provides an immutable record of transactions, enhancing security and reducing fraud risk. Clients benefit from greater transparency in their transactions.

5. **Positioning as a Market Leader**:
   - By embracing digital currencies and blockchain technology, JPMorgan has positioned itself as a leader in the financial industry, showcasing its commitment to innovation.

Future Directions

JPMorgan plans to expand the capabilities of JPM Coin by:

- Exploring its use in additional payment scenarios, including retail transactions and smaller-scale businesses.
- Continuing to enhance its blockchain infrastructure to support a wider range of digital currency applications.

- Collaborating with regulators and industry partners to develop standards for digital currency usage in the banking sector.

Conclusion

JPMorgan Chase's integration of digital currencies, particularly through the launch of JPM Coin, exemplifies the transformative potential of blockchain in modern finance. By streamlining payment processes, reducing costs, and enhancing security, the bank has not only improved its service offerings but also set a precedent for the broader adoption of digital currencies in the financial industry. This case study illustrates how embracing innovative technologies can drive significant improvements in traditional banking practices.

Made in United States
North Haven, CT
19 April 2025

68116249R00157